MODERNIZATION IN NEPAL

Modernization in Nepal

Edited by

B. R. BAJRACHARYA
S.R. SHARMA
S.R. BAKSHI

ANMOL PUBLICATIONS PVT LTD
New Delhi-110 002

ANMOL PUBLICATIONS PVT LTD
4374/4B, Ansari Road
Darya Ganj, New Delhi-110 002

First Edition, 1993

ISBN 81-7041-841-0

Printed in India

Published by J. L. Kumar for Anmol Publications Pvt. Ltd., New Delhi and Printed at Amit Enterprises, 518/14, Anup Market, Maujpur, Delhi.

Preface

Nepal is one of the developing societies to have started the process of modernization in the aftermath of the industrial revolution in Europe and the World War II. Till recently Nepal has been in the list of the least developed countries of the world. The monarchy freed itself from the clutches of the Rana family and this started a process of political modernization. Nepal has embarbed upon a planned economic development by adopting the five year plans. Around 1947 there was hardly any university in Nepal. Most of its colleges were affiliated to Patna University. But now a reasonable development of education in Nepal has taken place. The Panchayat System has given place to multiparty democracy in Nepal under the District Development Committee Act, 1992 has decided to divide the areas of 75 District Development Committees (DDC) of the kingdom of Nepal into the minimum of nine and maximum of seventeen at Ilakas.

In this book, the process of modernization in its historical perspectives has been analysed.

EDITORS

Contents

1

Political Modernization of Nepal

After the Emergence of Nepal as a nation-state in the last quarter of the eighteenth century, the primary goal of the Nepali political system became the maintenance of the status quo, which meant the continuation of the delicate balance of power among the various elite families composing the Court. The transfer of the capital from Gorkha to Kathmandu in 1769 gave added emphasis to the nationwide scope of the new political system, but did not result in any significant changes in the political process itself. The political system, like the social system at large, continued to be a highly segmented, pyramidal structure dominated by a handful of families belonging primarily to two castes—the Brahmans and the Kshatriyas. Members of these families supervised the functioning of the political system as part of the inherent rights emanating from their high-caste origins and reinforced by their traditions of familial service at the royal Court.

The traditional political system continued more or less intact until 1951. Whatever political changes occurred in the interim were largely systemic changes brought about by the redistribution of power among the elite families at the top of the political pyramid: the allocation of power among families and individuals changed, but the political system itself remained unchanged. Between 1770 and 1951, there were at least four momentous upheavals at the top level. In 1806, the Thapa family attained a virtual monopoly on political power; in 1846, the Rana family reached a similar position; in 1885, power shifted into the hands of the Shamsher branch of the Rana family; and in 1934, the A Rana group of the Shamsher Ranas came to the top. But none of these developments seriously affected the patterns, goals, or methods of the political system, since these families operated the administration during their tenure in office in more or less the same way, their overriding concern being invariably the enhancement of their material and political fortunes.

The familial basis of the traditional Nepali political system had a pervasive influence on all other organs of government, including the religious establishment, whose primary function was to provide a scriptural legitimation to the person or family in power. The machinery of administration was staffed along familial lines, and positions of power invariably corresponded to status earned by ascription rather than achievement. Similarly, the army was divided among various families or various branches of the same family, and the number of regiments assigned to a family became the most reliable index of its political power.

The Shah family occupied a pivotal position in the process of political change by virtue of its position as the sovereign power in Nepal. The elite families and the army swore ultimate allegiance to the head of the Shah family as the King of Nepal, and the common people, not directly involved in the process, accepted him as a reincarnation of Vishnu, the god of preservation in Hindu mythology. Indeed, the Shah King provided the only enduring basis of continuity and stability through all the complicated maneuvers and countermaneuvers of the elite families. The ruling family was, however, not itself immune to political ambitions, and its political activities were animated by the same spirit of familial gain as was typical of other elite families. Through all the vicissitudes of political change up to 1951, the Shah ruling family served as the ultimate custodian of authority and tradition and also as the ultimate source of all legitimizing powers required by the successive governments formed during this period.

THE NATURE AND CONTEXT OF CONTEMPORARY POLITICAL CHANGES

The political change resulting from the 1950 revolution was, on the other hand, a change *sui generis* which should not be equated with the earlier systemic changes. It was, rather, an extra systemic chance brought about by a fortuitous combination of external environmental conditiong—mainly, diplomatic pressure from India and the new spirit of political egalitarianism in Asia—and the activities of a newly emerging "modernizing" Nepali elite which had been educated in Western-style colleges and was alien to the traditional political system. King Tribhuwan was the only systemic agent involved in the change. But the role of the Shah monarch had been so effectively neutralized by the Rana regime that he could just as well be considered as standing outside the periphery of the operational political system and was in certain fundamental respects himself as extrasystemic as the new, modernizing elites. Moreover, his role in the 1950 revolution was more that of a catalyst rather than an active participant. His flight to the Indian Embassy in Kathmandu on November 6, 1950, and later his presence in New Delhi provided a diplomatic leverage to the Indian government in its negotiations with the Rana rulers of Nepal as well as a legitimizing basis for the anti-Rana activities of the Nepali agents of change—i.e., the Nepali Congress party.

The protracted negotiations in New Delhi, which preceded the 1951 political change, demonstrated the determining role of the Indian government and the diplomatic ineffectiveness of the family-centered Rana government. The Indian government was, presumably, representing the viewpoints of both King Tribhuwan and the Nepali Congress in the negotiations with the Rana government, but in reality both the King and the Nepali Congress were only minimally involved in these crucial discussions. Indeed, the Nepali Congress leaders were brought into the picture merely to ratify the agreement—later celebrated as the

Delhi compromise—which had been reached between the Indian and the Rana governments.

Thus, the political change which occurred in Nepal under the diplomatic midwifery of the Indian government was a total political change. It was neither an evolution from nor a modification of the traditional political system, but a brand-new innovation whose basic systemic linkages were with the emerging political structure in independent, democratic India. The Delhi compromise not only sounded the death knell of the Rana regime, but also, presumably, ruled out the viability of the traditional political process based on the dominance of a few elite families. Traditional political forms of action were to be superseded by political parties operating on a mass scale; representative democracy was solemnly affirmed as the goal of the new system; the election of a Constituent Assembly, to convene within two years, was envisaged; and the Crown was to function in a constitutional capacity as the symbol of national unity and solidarity far above the reaches of party politics. These new political concepts, which had previously existed only as vaguely defined theories in the minds of a new Nepalese educated in Western-style institutions, formed the basis of the 1951 Interim Government of Nepal Act—a hastily prepared adaptation of the 1950 Indian Constitution which was promulgated in Nepal with no evident concern for the lack of the prerequisites and concomitants which gave meaning to the Indian document.

The 1950 revolution was primarily an intellectuals' revolt against an archaic political system and involved the common people to only a limited degree, but its political aftermath was truly revolutionary and comparable to the effects of more comprehensive revolutions elsewhere. The political innovations introduced by the revolution were so sweeping, unfamiliar, and unprecedented that they were almost paralyzing in their immediate repercussions. None of the usual political infrastructure of a democratic system existed in Nepal; and the agents of the political change soon discovered the magnitude of the task involved in modernizing a basically medieval, feudal, castebound society. The entire administrative structure had to be innovated, and once again, since time was of the essence, the Indian model of bureaucracy was sought to be duplicated—in form, at least, if not in operation. The machinery of law and order had to be revamped, and the Indian government undertook the responsibility of reorganizing the police and the military along more modern lines. The bureaucracy, which had traditionally functioned as the custodian of law and order and as a managing agency for the ruling family, now had to add welfare and developmental activities to its functions, necessitating government expenditures on a broad variety of programmes. This led to a search for technical skills and economic aid from abroad, and again the Indian government was the first to respond with funds, plans, and programmes. Subsequently, other foreign governments responded and a new international image of Nepal camc into being.

The introduction of democratic experimentation in 1951 brought in its wake an array of new social and political roles for which there were few if any institutional or traditional supports in Nepal's society. Most of these were direct importations from India, where they had been nurtured under the long-sustained modernizing impact of British colonialism and had been strengthened by decades of anticolonial nationalist politics. Both these factors were conspicuously absent in Nepal; but the new political and administrative roles were tagged on, nonetheless, as an appendage of the incipient political system. Some examples of the new roles thus created were those of the political party leader, the public agitator, the opinion leader, the opposition leader, and the government official.

The newness of these roles stemmed directly from a modernist redefinition of the image of government in the body politic of the country. Traditionally, government in Nepal has been viewed by the people as an omnipotent agency of coercion led by men of inherently superior worth, who knew what was best for the country and whose actions were beyond the comprehension of the common man. The government functioned as an autochthonous institution at a respectable distance from the life-space of the people and made its presence felt only for such purposes as collecting taxes, settling litigations in the courts suppressing internal dissension, and resisting external aggression. Any public welfare activities, which were always infrequent, were widely publicized as symbolic of the regime's concern for the people, the objective being the enhancement of a benign, if authoritarian, "image" of the government.

When the new, modernizing educated elites assumed leading positions in the 1951 interim government, a revolutionary transformation of the image of government occurred. Political propagandists—including opposition leaders, newspaper editors, and pamphleteers—assiduously created the image of a new government that was no longer the master of the people, as it had been under the Ranas, but a conscientious servant of the people which had to be watched carefully for its acts of omission and commission. The public was cast in the unfamiliar role of critics and masters of the government; the high officials, who had traditionally been considered as objects of awe and reverence, were now described as public servants who could be dismissed outright if they acted against the interests of the people.

This new image of the government contradicted sharply with the *noblesse oblige* concept underlying the Shah or Rana systems of government. The traditional Nepali politician was an inveterate conspirator, one who operated in the deep, dark would of motives rather than overt actions, behind the scenes rather than in a public forum, and one whose public and private political lives were miles apart. Usually he was a "Court influential" who maintained his political preeminence by monopolizing all available channels of information for himself, thus depriving potential rivals of any knowledge other than routine information—often deliberately made misleading—of the crucial decisions under consideration. The Court influential endeared himself to the ruler and his family through a careful manipulation of information access and transmission, and his political fate was usually sealed when his opponents succeeded in establishing a more effective communication network in the Court.

After the 1951 political change, the inveterate conspirator was replaced by the public agitator, who took to street processions and public agitations rather than to palace cliques to advance his political goals. His policies and programmes had to be authenticated by opinion leaders, party followers, and the public before he could attain a position of prominence. In theory, the new political influential had to be a person who could mobilize maximum public support in his favour; in practice, however, the recognition of political popularity still had to be validated by a seal of approval from the royal palace. The newspaper editors and the pamphleteers replaced the informers and the rumor mongers of the traditional political system. But their mode of operation—scandalous gossip and character assassination against carefully selected targets—remained the same and provided the context for subsequent political changes. Youthful, inexperienced graduates of Western-style colleges replaced the old civil servants of the Rana regime in the key administrative positions in the new government, and a phenomenal expansion of the administrative staff filled up the scores of new positions in the civil service hierarchy.

The agents of political change, however, had failed to develop a consensus on the contours of the new political landscape that was to emerge in Nepal. The Nepali Congress leaders had acquired only a few years of political experience, and most of this time had been spent in trying to reconcile their individualistic orientation with the needs for corporate activity. As a result, a mature consensus on future political goals and programmes was not forthcoming among either the party leaders or the party rank-and file. The situation was further complicated by the sudden and unexpected collapse of the Rana regime, which found the party leaders unprepared and inadequately trained. Perhaps even more shattering were their experiences once they had taken the reins of administration, for they soon discovered that the governmental machinery that had seemed omnipotent from the outside was, when viewed from the inside and in its reality, quite weak and fragile.

The absence of a well-articulated ideology of political change not only hampered the activities of the government and the political parties, but also acted as a damper on the psychological atmosphere in Ncpal. The fall of the Rana regime produced initially a sense of popular exhilaration inspired by buoyant hopes of a political regeneration in the country and an impatient desire to "catch up" with the modern nations of the world. After a few months' experience with the new administration, the popular mood of exuberance underwent a perceptible change. A new political temper manifested itself, expecially in Kathmandu, in the form of cynical satirical, and often hostile evaluations of the political change and its multifaceted implications. Some Rana revivalists and their old allies sought to exploit this negative political mood in organizing opposition to the new political system. But even more dysfunctional than this Rana-inspired agitation was the conspicuous lack of ideologues, both among the public and in the political parties, who could serve as anchor men for the constantly-shifting, usually unrealistic expectations and moods of the people.

The inevitable outcome of this situation was the emergence of demagogues whose sole objective was the advancement of their personal political fortunes—even, if necessary, at the expense of the new system. This rise in political demagoguery and opportunism was also-attributable to the new ethics of public action, regarded at that time as the proper ideological accompaniment of parliamentary democracy, which underscored individualism as the fount of all political actions and ruled out familism as a basis for any corporate social or political activity.

Confusion concerning the nature and consequences of the 1951 political change was by no means limited to the general public. Indeed, there was a woeful lack of consensus among the political parties and their leaders as to what the change entailed in the social, economic cuitural, and educational processes of the country. The one common political denominator was a general awareness that the Rana regime in its historical form had ended; of interpretations and prognostications of the future political process there were as many as there were parties and leaders. The Rana revivalists and their followers foresaw the establishment of a Nepali Congress tyranny bolstered by massive support from India. The non-Rana, non-Communist political opposition also raised the specter of a dictatorial Nepal Congress regime. The handful of Communists interpreted the 1951 political change as a bourgeois revolution, characterized the Nepali Congress leadership as a "national-capitalist bourgeoisie," and laid out their own plans for the maturing of a "democratic" proletarian revolution in the future. A few obstreperous politicians who functioned in the guise of "independents" and loudly proclaimed their moral superiority to the party leaders viewed the change as the exclusive handiwork of Indian agents, Rana stooges, or a conspiracy between the Koirala brothers. Even the top-ranking Nepali Congress leaders did not share a common point of view on the nature of transitional politics and, in particular, on the role of the party in the ensuing interim period. This lack of ideological solidarity later proved to be the major cause of the repeated splintering of the party until finally in 1956 the Nepali Congress strengthened its ideological stance by adopting democratic socialism as its goal.

The lack of a well-articulated consensus about the 1951 political change revealed an ideolgical wasteland, in which the new, embryonic political system had to strike roots. It would have been a near miracle if the period of trial and error that ensued had produced a consensus which was lacking at the beginning of the new political era. This ideological deficit foretold the emergence of a modal political behaviour which would be guided more by pragmatic considerations of personal gain and convenience than by any fundamental commitment to political values.

POLITICAL ELITES

The traditional political elites of Nepal consisted primarily of a few Kshatriya and Brahman families having ancestral ties of kinship or service with the early Gorkha kingdom of the Shah rulers. The Brahmans functioned as a sacred elite and also had a monopoly of the legislative and judicial functions of the government, subject to the Shah ruler's veto. The Kshatriyas monopolized the executive branches of the government and filled key positions in the civil and military establishments. After power was seized in 1846 by a Kshatriya family later known as the Ranas, members of the Rana family monopolized all important positions in the government and the army, and a new sacred-elite Brahman family, subservient to the Rana regime, was created. Non-Rana political-elite families were largely liquidated; the few survivors among them were incorporated into the lower echelons of the Rana political system. Some of these families prospered under the Ranas and eventually regained an elite status. Most of them 'opposed the 1951 political change on pragmatic economic grounds rather than from any ideological attachment to the Rana system. Included within this category were non-Rana Kshatriyas, who abounded in the army, and Brahman and Newar families, who filled the second-level positions in the civil administration. Leading members of these families had acquired considerable property and wealth through their association with the Ranas and were, of course, opposed to the new spirit of economic egalitarianism. Subsequently, they became deeply involved in oppositional politics as "independents," as financial backers of opposition newspapers, and as self-appointed arbiters of interparty conflicts.

The new political elites which achieved prominence in the post-1951 period had mostly served an earlier political apprenticeship in India. They were drawn from a wide variety of Nepali ethnic groups, but their proportional representation in the new "modernizing" oligarchy was largely a reflection of the educational advancement of their respective communities. The ever resourceful Brahmans, who traditionally performed the intellectual functions in the Hindu social system, lost no time in becoming the avid patrons of the secular, liberal, Western-style educational system, in both Nepal and India. It is not surprising, therefore, that Brahmans constituted the largest single caste group in the new oligarchy and provided the core leadership for most political organizations and activities. Ethnic communities such as the Newers, Limbus, and Gurungs, which the Ranas had classified as Mongoloids and treated as second-class citizens, also were important among the new political elites. Their participation followed from their Western-style education or their exposure to modernizing influences in the British or Indian armies. Another important group, the inhabitants of the Terai, became active agents of political change because of their accessibility to educational facilities in India and their contacts with the Indian nationalist movement. They nursed a grievance of long standing for the discrimination practiced against the Terai plains dwellers as persons outside and even alien to the hill-dominated political structure.

The one underrepresented group in the new "modernizing" oligarchy was the Kshatriyas, who had usually been the principal agents of political change before 1951. Their situation is probably attributable to the extreme caution with which the Ranas had treated the non-Rana Kshatriyas, whom they regarded as their most dangerous political rivals, deliberately keeping them at a low educational level by providing places for them at the lower levels of the Rana system, particularly in the army. The only Kshatriyas directly involved in the 1951 political change were a few malcontent Ranas, Shahs, or Kshatriyas whom the Rana regime had failed, wittingly or unwittingly to accommodate.

In addition to their almost exclusively Indian political apprenticeship, the "modernizing" elite leaders shared other distinguishing characteristics. The great majority were educated in Western-style Indian schools and universities and to that extent shared some core values emphasizing the importance and dignity of the individual. Almost all of them believed that Nepal's salvation lay in modernization and industrialization rather than in some form of tradition-oriented political obscurantism. Even the few traditionalists among them—M P. Koirala, for example—had a basically modern definition of what was meant by tradition, favoured political secularism, and advocated such measures as separation of the religious establishment from the political process and modernization of the Nepali legal code. Another distinguishing characteristic was their comparative youthfulness, the great majority being in their twenties and thirties. In a country long dominated by old age, extended experience, and seniority of birth in its social and political systems, the youthfulness of the modernizers was symptomatic of the drastic challenge to authority and tradition embodied in the 1951 political change. There was an obvious generational conflict between the proponents of the new political order and the supporters of the Rana political system.

A characteristic of the new elites which had far-reaching political consequences was their extreme economic insecurity. Except for a few who were independently wealthy, the new leaders were usually persons of no economic substance or even fixed means of livelihood. In contrast to the British in India, the Rana regime had pursued so ruthless a policy of economic exploitation and political suppression that no middle class worthy of the name had emerged in Nepal. There were no professional groups, such as lawyers, doctors, or teachers, and no organized interest groups such as chambers of commerce, trade-unions, or landlord associations. In India, the leadership of the nationalist movement had been recruited mainly from the professional middle-class. In Nepal, leadership of the anti-Rana movement was mostly provided by members of emigre Nepali families who had been deprived of their traditional means of livelihood by the Ranas and who lived in India on a marginal subsistence basis. Thus, for most of the new elites, the pursuit of politics was not merely a means to an end, but an end in itself. For many, it became an exclusive profession, and economic affluence was directly dependent upon political survival. This situation helps explain the high incidence of opportunism in Nepali transitional politics. Leaders were often forced by sheer economic necessity to compromise their political idealism and pursue a politics of deception and short-term gains rather than of achievement and long-range goals.

The importance of the new political elites in the post-1951 reconstruction of the country was further accentuated because there were no technical elites to supplement and about their modernizing functions. Of the a handful of engineers, doctors, and educators in the entire country, most were concentrated in the capital. The Rana regime had discouraged the training of all technical elites except those connected with the army; and the few technicians tolerated by the regime to maintain the few appurtenances of the twentieth century in Nepal were required to play strictly subservient roles to the political masters of the Rana military establishment. Legend has it that the regime put to death a Rana engineer of high caliber for fear that his technical innovations would eventually prove to be a political menace to the regime.

In the face of the shortage of technicians and the inexperience of the new administrative class, the political elites frequently had to assume the roles of technicians and administrators when, in fact, the role they were most eligible to fill by virtue of their training and background was that of a literary elite. It is for this reason, presumably, that government policies and programmes were frequently imbued with metaphorical grandioseness and literary bombast rather than economic realism and technical precision.

All of the new political elites, whether or not they were systemic components of the traditional political system, could trace back their family history to some event in the past which had caused their dissatisfaction with the old system. These events, usually, were incidents of status withdrawal precipitated by political change; less frequently, they were associated with ideological revolt against the existing sociopolitical system. Two families which exerted important seminal influences on the maturing of the 1951 political change were the Koirala family of Biratnagar under the leadership of Krishna Prasad Koirala (the father of M.P. Koirala and B.P. Koirala) and the Joshi family of Kathmandu under the leadership of Madhava Raj Joshi (the father of Sukra Raj Shastri). These were both innovational families and the first generation of each paid a heavy price for its political or social nonconformity in the form of exile in India, economic hardships, and precarious existence. The Koirala family did the spade-work for the political change of 1951, and the Joshi family laid the background for a new social consciousness and ferment in Nepal through its advocacy of Hindu reform movements.

Of course, other Nepali families in the past had found themselves in conflict with the dominant political faction and sought asylum in India. But these had never been truly innovational families that contemplated major modification of the existing system. Their objective had usually been to introduce systemic changes in the political situation that would rebound to their advantage; they sought to replace the dominant political faction and retain the traditional system. These emigre families had gravitated, for the most part, to a few urban centers in India. The out-group Rana families usually made Calcutta their home-in-exile, while the Brahmanic ones tended to favour, Banaras, the holy city of the Hindus. In course of time these two Indian cities became centers of anti-Rana activity. The Banaras group eventually produced the Nepali National Congress and the Calcutta group the Nepal Democratic Congress. The fusion of these two groups into the Nepali Congress signified the emergence of a multifactional and, in *a* limited but meaningful sense, a national opposition to the Rana regime.

Although the emigre Nepali families maintained links with the larger Nepali society based in Kathmandu, the exigencies of foreign domicile their marginal means of livelihood, and their aversion to the rulers in Nepal endowed them in the course of time with cosmopolitan and sophisticated socio-political attitudes and beliefs. Countinued exposure to the varied political ideologies that were flourishing in India, particularly in Calcutta, and participation in the Indian nationalist struggles gave them a political perspective broader than that of the elites in Kathmandu, who had usually a very restricted political socialization. The non-Rana political elites in Kathmandu were largely by-products of the last Rana rulers' reluctant concessions to modernization—a few schools and hospitals intended as a veneer for obsolete political and administrative practices. Thus, the Kathmandu elites had grown up within the framework of the traditional familial and social systems. They were, therefore, far more exposed to the authoritarianism typical of the Nepali familial system than their cosmopolite counterparts in Banaras or Calcutta, and were also obligated to display greater conformity in their social and political behaviour. Their oppositional politics had to be conducted with extreme caution and deliberateness since the risks they were cowting wre infinitely greater.

This significant difference in political socialization between the Nepali political elites in Banaras and Calcutta and those in Kathmandu produced a fundamental split in the post-1951 political process that had an enduring effect. The cosmopolites attained positions of political power-in 1951 on the basis of their role in expertise stemming from their broad experiences in Indian movements. The Kathmandu elites reached by accusing the Banaras and Calcutta groups of worming their way into positions of power with the support and blessings of the Indian government. They claimed that they alone were eligible to guide the processes of government during the transitional period since they, in contrast to most of their cosmopolite rivals, possessed the most significant political credential—that is, status as "political sufferers" owing to several years' incaceration in Rana jails. In Nepal, as in India after independence, the primary criteria for political leadership were not training or competence but personal suffering and self-abnegation in the service of a cause. There would seem to be here a reflection of that ideal of Hindu society which glorified the *sadhu,* who had renounced worldly possessions and personal desires and taken to a life of other-worldly contemplation, as the ideal person. In some respects, the ideal political leader was expected to pattern himself after the sadhu in his personal conduct and political behaviour.

POLITICAL PARTIES: IDEOLOGY AND COMPOSITION

The political parties were in most cases combinations of elite groups on such bases as friendship ties, and, less frequently, ideological commitments. The elitist nature of political organizations increased the likelihood of leadership conflicts and realignments and complicated the establishing of a mass basis for party activities. This feature highlighted the importance of a few persons who were prominent in other public activities as well as politics. Several of the social and cultural organizations that cropped up in such profusion after 1951 were the creations of political leaders. This interlocking pattern of leadership in public affairs accounts for the overwhelming importance of the *homo politicus* in contemporary Nepal.

Since most of the new political elites professed more or less identical philosophies of modernization and development, their political slogans and mostrums were broadly similar. The single exception was the Communist Party of Nepal, which had a prefabricated ideology and was, therefore, excluded from the typical ideological groupings. The rest of the parties concocted virtually identical manifestoes specifying their objectives and programmes. This was particularly noticeable during the 1959 general elections, when the choice available to the voter was essentially between the personal reputations of the candidates rather than their party ideologies or affiliations. The differences between the contending parties were usually those of points of emphasis or the idiosyncratic predilections of a few individual politicians.

Inasmuch as the behaviour of the politicai elites was governed in part by a new ethics of individualism acquired in the process of education at Western-style institutions, their party conflicts and tussles were also imbued with the same spirit. Political opponents, both within a party or in other parties, were designated as traitors to the cause. In support of such charges, insinuations of connections with a foreign government or reactionary elements were usually circulated. When such charges were implausible or unconvincing, the object of the abuse was instead excoriated for violations of party rules and procedures and was sometimes excommunicated from the organization. The activities of the careerists among the political elites often seemed to alternate between impugning the motives of their rivals and denouncing their allegedly unconstitutional acts. In any case, this proclivity for verbal abuse made a substantial contribution to the unstable, yet dynamic nature of the politics of the transitional period.

The rank and file of the political parties was largely recruited from such groups as students, the literati, merchants, former servicemen of the British and Indian armies, and urbanized peasants. In the few urban areas of Nepal, and notably Kathmandu, the introduction of the party system had an unexpected socializing effect in that it helped transform erstwhile unruly, antisocial elements into respectable political leaders. Some of these men even had criminal records and were best known earlier for their propensity for street fighting and other antisocial activities during the celebration of folk festivals. But after 1951, they became party faithfuls and their gangs attained an important status as pressure groups in the various parties. This easy induction of marginal groups into the new political process underscores the innovational aspect of the 1951 politicai change in Nepal.

Regionally, most of the rank and file of the political parties was either from the Terai or from Kathmandu Valley. These were politically the most advanced areas in Nepal, and the immediate impact of the 1951 political change was most acutely felt there. With the exception of the Communists, the parties recruited members in a relatively free and open manner. No severe tests of party loyalty or ideological firmness were imposed; and often the rank and file crossed party lines in conjunction with the political maneuvers of their selected leaders. Owing to the undeveloped state of transportation and communication facilities, most party headquarters—usually set in Kathmandu—were unable to exercise adequate control over their branch organizations in the districts. Consequently the branches' activities were typically characterized by a degree of autonomy which was seldom conducive to party strength or unity.

Given the elitist background of party leadership and the composition of the rank and file, it was comparatively easy in the new political context for any sufficiently motivated person to establish a party of his own. The one crucial element was the creation of an effective communication system through such measures as frequent public meetings and processions and, most important, by launching a vigorous and sensational party propaganda campaign. In the years following-1951 the printing presses and public-address systems in the capital were constantly in demand. Scores of party publicity bulletins, newspapers, monthlies, and annuals were launched. None of these publications attained mass circulation proportions. even in the Nepali context. The most widely read probably did not have a circulation exceeding two thousand. Nevertheless, the sum total of this massive scale of publications was a revolution in the Kathmandu communication pattern. This continues to be a special characteristic of the capital even today, although with the emergence of Radio Nepal and the improvement in transportation facilities, communication on a national scale isdeveloping gradually.

The inflation of the communication process in the new political system was also a reflection of the fact that the representative status of the political parties was not tested for nearly seven years by the one universally applicable standard—free elections. In this interim period, any party which could whip up noisy political support in Kathmandu had a good chance of gaining political influence at the royal palace and, thereby, ministerial posts in the government. This explains why a few relatively unrepresentative parties and political leaders, with a communication system that gained attention in places where it mattered the most, were able to continue in power for extended periods.

One characteristic of the new political communication system was the tendency for the contents not to conform to facts and events. Typically, the newspapers and other publicity media placed more emphasis on opinions, judgments, interpretations, and rumors than on straightforward and factual reporting of events. Excessive attention to what was factual did not fit into the prevailing political ethos—and also often hurt rather than helped the already precarious financial condition of a newspaper. It can be argued that the development of a modern communication system in Kathmandu using the printed word rather than the word of mouth did little to improve the factual basis for political activity, and only accelerated the tempo of political life with the aid of modern technology.

In this context, one institution which attained an elite political status despite its not having the form of a political party was the Palace Secretariat. Because of its strategic location in the new political process, it became the procurer, purveyor, and censor of all communications channeled to the King for his information in making a decision. The criteria used by the palace staff in screening public information for presentation to the King and the biases in their selections presumably have influenced both the immediate and the long-range future of the country. That King Mahendra has, however, used various techniques to validate reports received through the vested interests—inspired communication network of the Palace Secretariat is evidenced by his establishing direct links with the people on his walking tours and public appearances throughout the country and by his care in soliciting the views of most important political factions on issues under consideration.

It is still unclear what role the Palace Secretariat staff played in bringing about the political crisis of December, 1960, which as an event was primarily a spectacular breakdown in communication between King Mahendra and the Nepali Congress government, especially its Prime Minister. As the authority of the elected government constituted both an ideological and political challenge to the extraparliamentary jurisdiction of the Palace Secretariat, there are grounds for assuming that the latter was responsible for the breakdown in communication.

The insistent current demand of the "partyless" members of the present Council of Ministers in Nepal that only those who support their political actions are patriots and that those who are critical or even vaguely indifferent to them are necessarily traitors and "antinationals" is yet another index of a one-sided political communication system. A country in which economic development is the prime target can ill afford to lose national consensus and unity—the most valuable "capital" of a poor country—in order to insure the continuation of a few politicians in power. A national unity of purpose and a national consensus of ideology are not born out of political legerdemain or slogan making, but out of a spirit of national participation freely volunteered and constructively used. Any attempt to fabricate an artificial national consensus by such means as coercion, political blackmail, and a manipulated press may be temporarily expedient, but in the long run it is likely o prove self-defeating and destructive of national interests. In the final analysis, the creation of a democratic, modern political system—the stated objective of Panchayat Raj—is nothing more than the creation of a participant society in which each individual or class takes part freely and productively in the affairs of that society. King Mahendra's formulation of the goals of panchayat democracy seems to be based on a similar vision. The translation of these goals into accomplisnments is the continuing political preoccupation in Nepal.

POLITICAL PARTIES: TYPOLOGY AND DESCRIPTION

As noted earlier, the political parties in Nepal have had only superficial differences in their policies and programmes. A meaningful typology of the parties, therefore, would have to be based on certain nonideological characteristics of their core leadership rather than on trivial and idiosyncratic differences. The core leadership in any party is that particular collection of persons which has been instrumental in the founding of the group and in sustaining and continuing it through changing political alignments and subsequentfragmentations. The essential novelty of the 1951 political change was that it provided for a new mode of interpersonal relationship in a society which traditionally had sanctioned corporate activity. whether political or social, only along familial or caste lines and related lines of friendship or dependency. The commitment to political change can, therefore, be judged by the nature and stability of the interpersonal relations which characterized the original core leadership of the political parties. In addition, a typology accounting for the organization and disorganization of the parties can be formulated on this basis.

The core leadership of the political parties basically committed to the 1951 political change was multi-ethnic and multifamilial—in short, national—in contrast to that of parties only peripherally or opportunistically committed to political innovations. The leadership of this latter group of parties was based either on the traditional or conventional patterns of interpersonal relationships or on common allegiance to an authoritarian personality.

The qualitative difference in commitment to the 1951 political change also provides a non-ideological definition of modernists as opposed to traditionalists. A modernist's political behaviour would depart sharply from tradition since it would be governed largely by an enduring multi-ethnic, multifamilial consensus within the top echelons of party leadership; a traditionalist's political behaviour, on the other hand, would fail within the traditional sanctions for corporate activity such as familial ties, caste, and friendship or dependent relationships. Most political splinter groups that arose in Nepal after the 1950 revolution were essentially authoritarian groups led by a factional leader with the support of small cliques, and were also the most active participants in political alliances and schisms.

The accompanying tabulation presents a typology of political parties in Nepal based on the characteristics of their core leadership.

INTEREST GROUPS AND PRESSURE GROUPS

The traditional Nepali political system developed out of a long-term (if not always peaceful) balancing of the interests of four prominent groups—the royal family, the sacred elite, the military, and the landowing aristocracy. These interest groups usually effected political changes through their participation in or association with the Court—whether Shah or Rana. The 1951 political change did not alter this basic pattern of traditional politics, but only pushed it into the background—temporarily, it turned out—as new interest groups and pressure groups intruded on the political scene, bearing contemporary labels and using a modern political vocabulary.

The new interest groups were the Crown, in its modernized form; the "modernizing" oligarchy; merchants and businessmen; and the political party leaders. The pressure groups through which they sought to exercise influence were the press, student organizations, administrative positions, the party system, and various social and cultural bodies. Among the traditional interest groups, the sacred elite and the military

TABLE 1.1

A Typology of Political Parties Participating in the 1959 General Elections in Nepal

Modern	Traditional
Nepali Congress	Nepal Praja Parishad (Tanka Prasad Acharya faction)
Core leadership: B. P. Koirala, Suvarna Shamsher, Ganesh Man Singh, S.P. Upadhyaya	*Core leadership*: Tanka Prasad Acharya, Rama Hari Sharma, Chuda Prasad Sharma
Composition: Two Brahmans, one Kshatriya, one Newar	*Composition*: Three Brahmans
Classification: National	*Classification*: One caste friendship clique
Nepal Gorkha Parishad	Nepal Praja Parishad (B. Mishra faction)
Core leadership: Mrigendra Shamsher, Bharat Shamsher, Ranadhir Subba, Deva Bir Pande	*Core leadership*: B. Mishra Composition: One Terai Brahman
Composition: Two Kshatriyas, one Brahman, one Limbu	*Classification*: One-personality party
Classification: Originally familial, later national	United Democratic party
Communist Party of Nepal	*Core leadership*: K.I. Singh
Core leadership: Pushpa Lal, Manmohan Adhikari, Tulsi	Composition: One hill Kshatriya
Lal, Keshar Jang Raymajhi	*Classification*: One-personality party
Composition: Two Newars, one Brahman, one Kshatriya	Nepal Terai Congress

<table>
<tr>
<td>*Classification*: Originally ethnic, later national</td>
<td>*Core leadership*: V. Jha
Composition: One Terai Brahman
Classification: One personality party
Nepali National Congress
Core leadersheip: D. R. Regmi
Composition: One Kathmandu Brahman
Classification: One-personality party
Nepal Prajatantrik Mahasabha
Core leadership: Ranga Nath Sharma
Composition: One Brahman
Classification: One personality party</td>
</tr>
</table>

played a fairly dormant role until December, 1960, but the landowning aristocracy continued to play an important and active role in the guise of nonparty "independent" politicians. The crushing defeat suffered by the independents in the 1959 general elections forced them to change their tactics and resort to organized opposition to the Nepali Congress. With the assistance of some commercial interests, they formed the Jana Hita Sangh to oppose the land rcform and taxation policies of the Nepali Congress Government.

The 1951 political change also provided the conditions under which a multitude of occupational organizations, ranging from a tailors' union to a school teachers' association, were established. In most instances, these vocational groups were ill prepared to defend and promote their specialized interest; some, like the drivers' union exerted most of their energy in political activities that often seemed far removed from the nominal objectives of the organization. In general, the occupational groups failed to make a significant impression on the politics of the transitional period, with the possible exception of the Kisan Sangh, a Communist controlled peasant organization. Since 1961 some of the occupational groups have been combined into a few government-sponsored class organizations, but this has not as yet noticeably increased their effectiveness as pressure groups.

The Crown's Role in Transitional Politics

After the overthrow of the Rana regime, the Crown became the symbol of national awakening and unity. King Tribhuwan was acclaimed as a liberator for his support of the anti-Rana revolution and as the "father of the nation" and "architect of democracy" after his restoration. During his reign the nonpolitical character of the Crown was widely publicized, although at the same time the failures of the successive political experiments rendered the Crown the most powerful political institution in the country.

King Mahendra's accession to the throne in March, 1955, marked a further stage in the evolution of the Crown's political role. The new King took a direct interest in politics and the government of the country and created a dynamic image of the Crown as an active agent in the political realm by undertaking extensive travels throughout the country, engaging in protracted negotiations with political parties, and experimenting with new administrative and political institutions. Thus the Crown not only superseded the traditional role of the Rana Prime Minister, but acquired new roles befitting the exigencies of the transitional politics. In the process the Crown also became the focus around which traditional interest groups such as the sacred elite, the military, and the landowning aristocracy pivoted. These groups found access to the royal palace through their supporters and representatives on the staff of the Palace Secretariat.

Since December, 1960, the Crown has been directly involved in the establishment and functioning of the new political system, Panchayat Raj, which is often described by official sources as an "absolute" system for which there is no replacement. This equation of the Crown with the panchayat system exposes the former to unnecessary political risks and may well prejudice the long-range interest of both the Crown and the country by seeming to imply that each is dependent upon the other for its own survival. The political system of any backward, underdeveloped country is, by definition, tentative. It is both unrealistic and dangerous, therefore, to think in terms of "ideal" political systems at this stage when changes in Nepal's economic, social, and educational systems will inevitably lead to correlated changes and adjustments in the political structure.

The "Modernizing" Oligarchy

The "modernizing" oligarchy which provided the initiative for the 1951 political change and the transitional politics thereafter was the most inchoate and disorganized of the articulate political groups in Nepal. Members of the group were active in forming political parties, starting newspapers, staffing educational institutions, and providing administrators for the new government. But owing to their essentially individualistic outlook and highly personalized interpretations of modernization and change, they were fragmented into numerous small groups and coteries, including political parties, and were never in a position to influence developments as a collective entity.

In addition to political parties, three pressure groups emerged from the "modernizing" oligarchy—the student organizations, the journalists, and the civil service. The students were the best organized and, hence, the group whose support was most eagerly solicited. The agitational activities of political parties, for instance, were largely dependent upon student participation. The journalists—in particular, the "independents"—were usually strong critics of any government in power as the voice of a highly emotional Nepali nationalism and as supporters of the landowning aristocracy, members of which were in most cases their behind-the-scenes financiers.

The new class of administrators emerged as a pressure group in the 1951-59 period primarily as a reaction to the insecurity of tenure at the Central Secretariat and their uneasy relationship with their political bosses—the Ministers. In their search for stability and security they tended to look toward the palace for support and to favour royal intervention in the processes of government. Upon the installation of an elected government in 1959, the administrative machinery was revamped to suit the purposes and procedures of a parliamentary form of government. The comparative stability and expected longevity of the Nepali Congress regime encouraged important elements of the administrative elite to shift their attention from the royal palace to the Ministry, and the role of the administrators as a pressure group encouraging royal participation in politics was temporarily suspended. It was for this reason, presumably, that a wholesale purge was conducted at both the central and the district administrative level after December, 1960, so as to reinsert into the upper-level positions administrators whose personal careers were closely interlinked with the fortunes of the royal palace.

Creation of new Interest Groups Under the Panchayat System

The panchayat political experiment in Nepal has involved setting up several new political institutions to replace the banned political parties. Significant among them are the several government-sponsored "class" organizations, which in effect are designed to be nationwide interest groups. The activities of these new groups are still largely programmatic, and it remains to be seen how effectively they can serve their intended purposes in the new political context. One important factor which reduces their effectiveness is the fact that many former political party members, indoctrinated and ingrained in a decade of active party politics, have joined these "nonparty" institutions at both the leadership and the rank-and-file levels. The presence of these people has brought in the spirit of party politics, thus compromising the official message of partyless democracy. Additionally, these various interest groups cannot avoid competing against each other to promote their respective interests. This situation is tantamount to a revival of factional politics and could become more disruptive and antinational than the political party system at its most opportunistic level of operation.

THE NATURE OF TRANSITIONAL POLITICS

In the preceding section a distinction was made between traditional and modern political parties, using a particularistic-universalistic dichotomy to analyze the relationship underlying the composition of their core leadership. The distinction was found to be both conceptually and empirically meaningful in explaining the differences in their activities. It is now to be seen how transitional politics unfolded through the years within the context of tradition-based attitudinal and behavioral constraints and under the impact of an imported ideology of modernization. The underlying conflict between tradition and modernity gave an indigenous motive force to transitional politics. The absence of clear-cut alien traditions which needed uprooting or, at least, absorption into a new political system brought to the surface the affective or expressive part of the conflict rather than its problemsolving aspects.

In contrast to India, there were no vestiges of foreign rule to erase and no alien cultural legacies to liquidate or assimilate. Despite their tyrannical record, the Ranas were still Nepalese, and their regime was so quickly dismantled that anti-Rana slogans had become superfluous by the end of 1951. Even the handful of non-Rana supporters of the Rana political system were quickly rehabilitated politically. The lack of a foreign scapegoat imparted an inwardness to political conflicts from the very outset. Motives or the interpretations of motives of the political participants were considered more important than their actions as the crucial variables in the political process.

Traditionally, Nepali society granted status to its members strictly on the basis of such ascriptive considerations as caste, ancestry, and connections of kinship or familial service with the elite families. The striving for and maintenance of status was the fundamental motivation of all public activities. A man of status was eligible for almost all positions of power in the society, whether or not he had any specialized skills. Most of the new political elites that emerged after 1951 were profoundly affected by the same traditional concern for status, as was reflected in their readiness to pay any political price to achieves ministerial rank. The search for status among the politicians- was only hypothetically based on "modern" concepts of achievement considerations; for the most part, high government offices were sought and distributed as royal favours on the basis of political influence rather than achievement, as the political elites fully understood. In theory, however, the political elites had accepted the concept of an egalitarian society which would break down artificial barriers of status, caste, and other social inequalities and would emphasize personal achievements rather than connections as the basis for advancement. This divorce of practice from theory was most perceptible in the recruitment of the administrative cadres, which was usually effected on the basis of personal or party connections, but was usually rationalized in terms of achievement. The record of the Public Service Commission, which served more as an agency for administrative ritualism than as a proper invigilatory body, is an eloquent tribute to this state of affairs during the transitional period.

There was—and is—a high degree of ritualization in Nepali social life, and the transitional politics also easily acquired similar ritualistic aspects. The Nepali view of the world traditionally had been marked by an absence of causality, rationationality, and predictability, especially as it referred to the political and the physical world. As corollaries to such a belief system, elaborate rituals had been created as a protection against unforeseen events, and the role of astrologers as the most important technicians in the country had been institutionalized. Each of the elite families, including the royal family, had its own consulting astrologer, who recommended propitiatory rites when his clients were in distress or danger and auspicious moments for every ritual or new undertaking.

The introduction in 1951 of a political system with implicit biases of rationality in the allocation and legitimation of power ran directly counter to the pervasive astrological frame of reference of Nepali society. It was perhaps inevitable under such circumstances that the new political system would operate in an irrational and unpredictable manner, producing many surprises and uncertainties in the process—of which, the establishment of K.I. Singh's government in July, 1957, and its abrupt dissolution three months later was the most striking example.

The period of transitional politics was thus a period of profound anxiety, uncertainty, and tension in Nepal's public life, revealed in stresses of various kinds in the body politic of the country. At the cognitive level, there was widespread confusion among the political parties and the public; as to the meaning of political democracy; at the emotional level, there was mounting frustration caused by the increasing awareness that the new political system was not the panacea that it had been claimed to be; at the behavioural level, there was a bedlam of confusion and conflict resulting from the free-wheeling enactment of roles imported from abroad and imprecisely defined for the Nepali environment.

The result of this ideological, attitudinal, and behavioural confusion was that Nepali political elites became preoccupied with self-expression rather than with problem solving. The leaders fluctuated uneasily between feelings of omnipotence and impotence; they refused to bow to the discipline of facts, and were more concerned with striking the appropriate political pose than with carrying out a particular course of action. The political process. in turn, became marked by vacillations between extended periods of inaction and short periods of frantic action. Every time there was a Cabinet crisis, all political parties responded to the opportunities inherent in the situation by frantic and noisy demonstrations of their political "high caste," as it were; at other times they engaged in subterranean, tortuous political maneuvers and countermaneuvers to bring about the fall of existing governments. These unstable, demoralizing transitional politics would have been terminated much sooner if the political parties had co-operated and made a concerted effort to hold the general elections as quickly as possible. But the zigzag nature of transitional politics had been so rewarding and promising to the inbred and self-centered political elites that the majority of them sought instead to prolong this period as long as possible.

The course of transitional politics in Nepal from 1951 to 1959 is essentially the career of a political innovation from its initiation through various stages of modification to its culmination. The period of transition was crammed with political activities relating to the adaptation and modification of the innovation. From February, 1951, to March, 1955, King Tribhuwan and the political elites experimented with various governments in the hope that the new political system would somehow be acculturated to Nepali conditions. But the fragmentation of the political elites into many opposing camps, the King's deteriorating health, the lack of institutional supports for new political roles, and the rise of an organized group that rejected the 1951 political change helped to dislocate political innovation patterned after that of neighbouring India. Governments formed between 1951 and 1955 were so preoccupied with problems relating to their political survival that they ignored their task orientation almost completely and failed, in the words of King Mahendra, to produce even "four tangible examples of achievement." Popular expectations of rapid progress and development in the country after the overthrow of the Rana regime were thwarted, and the initial fund of public good-will for the political innovation had all but disappeared by March, 1955.

It was on the ground that so-called democratic party governments had failed to deliver the goods to the people that King Mahendra launched another political innovation—amounting almost to a counter-innovation to the 1951 political change—when he ascended the throne in March, 1955. His new political approach was heavily task-oriented, and the new political experiments he introduced were based on a dynamic political role for the Crown, limited participation by the political parties (in the belief that party politics was more conflict-oriented than task-oriented), and a hypothetical commitment to democratic values King Mahendra's extensive tours outside Nepal undoubtedly impressed on him the medieval backwardness of his country as well as the need for an accelerated development programme. They also perhaps reinforced his conviction that party politics in Nepal was too divisive, personality-centered, and conflict-ridden to be suitable as a means of rapid modernization.

The rise of an indigenous innovation in the form of King Mahendra's dynamic political role received wide support from all those elements which had found the 1951 political change not to their taste. They would have preferred to abandon the so-called democratic experiment completely and immediately, and would have supported revival of the traditional, if benevolent despotism of the Shah rulers. But King Tribhuwan's memory was still fresh in the people's minds, and the early abandonment of parliamentary democracy, which was still acclaimed as his creation, would have been construed as a betrayal of his legacy and an insult to his memory.

Thus, the period from 1955 to 1959 was marked by several compromises with the aims of the 1951 political change and a continuous modification of the interim constitutional system so as to accommodate the new political role of the Crown.

This period was also marked by the emergence of a new class of politicians—the court influentials—who acted as political brokers for King Mahendra's counter-innovations. These elements prepared the ideological and emotional background for the eventual abolition of parliamentary democracy. More concretely, they injected a new public controversy by propounding the thesis that the long overdue general elections should be held for a Parliament and not a Constituent Assembly and that King Mahendra should bestow a Constitution on the people. These proposals directly contradicted King Tribhuwan's Royal Proclamation of February 18, 1951, and were based on two assumptions concerning the political process in the country namely, that sovereignty in the country resided not in the popular wlll but in the King, and that the people of Nepal at the present stage of the country's development were incapable of governing themselves and required guidance and supervision from higher authorities.

The debate between the proponents of Constituent Assembly or Parliament raged for nearly two years and divided the political parties and elites neatly into two categories—those who operated on the Indian model and were committed to the aims of the 1950 revolution, and those who opposed the Indian model, criticized Indian influence in Nepal, and were committed to the espousal of King Mahendra's innovations. King Mahendra finally decided the controversy on February 1, 1958, in favour of a Parliament. Subsequently, on February 12, 1959, he approved and bestowed a Constitution on the country. The first general elections commenced a week later, and the period of transitional politics was officially terminated on June 30, the day the new Constitution went into effect and the first elected constitutional government formed by the Nepali Congress was established.

POLITICAL MODERNIZATION: PARLIAMENTARY DEMOCRACY VERSUS PANCHAYAT DEMOCRACY

The establishment of a parliamentary type of government in 1959 and the introduction of a panchayat form of government in 1962 must both be viewed as attempts to bring about the rapid modernization of the country by institutional measures rather than by the long-drawn-out process of developing the correlates of modernization. None of the usual indicators of modernization were present in Nepal when the country broke from its centuries-old geographical and political insulation in 1951. The national rate of literacy was below 5 per cent; industrialization amounted to no more than a handful of factories in the Terai under the entrepreneurship of Indian businessmen; communications and transport facilities were at a primitive stage of development; religion had not been separated from the functions of government; there had been no broadening of the so-called middle-class groups; there was no increasing mobility in social; vocational, and geographical spheres; contractually organized limited interest associations were non-existent; scientific and engineering achievements were conspicuous by their absence. In brief, the task of modernizing Nepal was of truly Herculean proportions, involving the revamping of a medieval, disease-ridden, illiterate, poor, and backward country into a modern, national society. Political modernization in such a context meant a revolutionary change in the form and functions of the government, directed toward the creation of a participant society; administratively, it meant an ever growing expansion in the scope of governmental activity; economically, it meant the mobilization of all available internal resources and all procurable foreign assistance to meet the enormous costs of modernization.

During the years of transitional politics (1951-59) only four significant modernization measures materialized. The most important was a phenomenal expansion in educational facilities all over the country, mostly on the initiative of the local communities Many schools and colleges were established, and the number of students enrolled in various educational institutions increased tremendously. Second, there was a modernization of the army, under the supervision of the Indian Military Mission. The reorganization of the army took some six years to complete, and its costs told heavily on the slender resources of the successive governments, each of which allocated to it a substantial proportion—at times more than 50 per cent—of the total budget. Third, there was the completion of the first modern highway linking Kathmandu with India and the construction of a modern airport at the capital. It is noteworthy that both the modernization of the army and the construction of the Nepal-India road were possible during the transitional years only because the Indian government took the sole responsibility for these projects as both financier and contractor for the Nepal government. Finally, the Nepal government succeeded in projecting a new image on the world scene and was able to secure technical and economic assistance from several foreign countries, including India, the United States, the Soviet Union, Communist China, and the United Nations. In fact, the volume of foreign aid reached proportions that the unstable administrative apparatus of the country could not absorb and utilize, and economic development was seriously impeded by a faltering administrative machinery, which reflected the weak, unstable political structure in the country.

The establishment of a strong, elected parliamentary form of government in May, 1959, marked the end of the inchoate transitional politics and the introduction of a confident, vigorous political structure for the first time since 1951. It was widely expected that the missing ingredient of political stability which had hampered reforms in the economic and administrative systems in the preceding years, was finally restored. A long overdue sense of popular optimism was reborn. The new government, embarking upon its modernization programme with zeal and vigor, sought to introduce all the textbook features of a modern polity—such as a highly differentiated and functionally specific system of governmental organization, integration withln the governmental structure, rational and secular procedures for making political decisions, popular interest and involvement in the political system, and judicial processes based on a secular and impersonal system of law. The administrative services were codified and regularized; the legal system was expanded and modernized; the feudal land system was modified; government revenues were replenished by the imposition of income taxes and property taxes: and the implementation of development projects was accelerated.

But the activities of the elected Nepali Congress government placed it directly in opposition to all those elements which had dominated transitional politics from 1955 to 1959 and which had been routed nearly out of political existence in the general elections of 1959. All these elements magnified the threat of the new political system to King Mahendra's innovation of a dynamic role for the Crown. The Nepali Congress leaders of the elected government, misjudging the situation, overlooked the important fact that the 1959 Constitution did not in fact provide for the democratic political system under which they presumed they were operating. Most of them had been politically socialized in India, and they conducted themselves in their political roles as if they were operating under the 1950 Indian Constitution. Thus discrepancies between their performance and their role definitions as provided under the 1959 Nepal Constitution were inevitable, and the accumulation exploded finally into the political crisis of December 15, 1960, when King Mahendra swiftly, abruptly, and unceremoniously scuttled the experiment in parliamentary government and resumed his own political innovations, which had been suspended during the parliamentary interlude.

All through 1961 King Machendra searched for an ideology that would serve not merely as a replacement for parliamentary government but also as a culmination of the innovational process he had introduced in 1955 in the form of a dynamic, authoritarian, politically oriented monarchy. This was finally accomplished through the promulgation of the 1962 Constitution and the inauguration of the National Panchayat in 1963. It is interesting to note that the democratic label is still in wide use in Nepal. Often the present political system is alluded to as panchayat democracy. The use of the term "panchayat" is intended, presumably, to attribute an indigenous and traditional character to the new political system. Except for the attribution, however, all the various bodies that are being established as part of the panchayat system are as a historical in Nepal as was the Parliament under the 1959 Constitution. The real rationale of the panchayat system is political rather than ideological or traditional. It is based on a teleological concept of democracy which assumes that the Nepali people are unprepared for autonomous political action except at the lowest levels of task complexity and that the constituted authority—that is, the King—holds ultimate responsibility for the determination of the country's political system.

At the highest level of the political process, the King and his advisers have wide discretionary powers for political decision, and they alone are responsible for articulating the goals of national politics. The so-called decentralization of powers within the panchayat system has provided zonal, district, and local institutions with some degree of autonomy in local administration—but at the price of a complete segregation from national politics. Indeed, one potential danger inherent within the panchayat system is the possibility that concern with local and parochial issues may usurp the importance of national consensus and solidarity in a country which is already saddled with dangerous tradition-based social, ethnic, linguistic, and regional divisions.

The panchayat regime can conceivably be a more effective agent of modernization than parliamentary democracy in some areas of national life. By eliminating the element of competitive politics from Nepali public life, it has made room for speedy implementation of decisions handed down from above. It may have "toned up" the administrative machinery to some extent through the use of such negative incentives as fear of outright dismissals, for even the highest officials cannot be immune from the feeling that they are under the constant scrutiny of the palace. This technique of administrative control was used with considerable success by the Rana regime and may still be effective for directing some categories of present-day administrative personnel. But it is still uncertain what role the administration would play if a serious challenge to the regime should emerge.

The panchayat regime has continued the economic and land-reform measures of its predecessor with only a few minor changes. It is only in the areas of social legislation and foreign affairs that it has some significant achievements to its credit. King Mahendra's promulgation of a new legal code in 1963, banning many discriminatory social practices, marks an important milestone in the social development of the country; it also underscores the point that it is much easier to change some aspects of a traditional society through the application of force than by persuasion. In the realm of foreign affairs, King Mahendra has scored some personal triumphs, though it remains to be seen whether his current diplomatic successes will have enduring value both for his political career and the future of the country. By pursuing a policy of equal friendship with both China and India, and a policy of neutrality in the Himalayan border disputes and armed conflicts between its two neighbours, Nepal has, at least, temporarily received concessions from both sides. On the international scene, King Mahendra projected a new, magnified image of Nepal by personally participating in the Belgrade conference of neutral countries in 1961 and by undertaking extensive tours of several foreign countries.

It is yet too early to forecast how well the new panchayat institutions and class organizations are going to function in Nepal and how effective they are going to be in the process of rapid modernization. The National Panchayat has not achieved a significant role for itself as yet, and the government is still experimenting with the delegation of administrative authority to the local panchayats. Both parliamentary government and panchayat government can be viewed as more or less tentative political instruments of stimulated change. The first sought to promote change by seeking the consent and the participation of the people in the change process, and the latter seeks to promote change by means of directives issued from above on the assumption that the linking of authority with change will accelerate the change process in a traditional society such as that of Nepal. It is possible that the panchayat system, with all its inadequacies as an agent of change, is nevertheless the most viable political structure for contemporary Nepal precisely because it does remove the likelihood of a struggle between the Crown and the Ministry which could otherwise absorb all the attention and energies of the participants in the political process. The King's will reigns supreme and unchallenged under the panchayat system. If a Minister happens to be out of step with the royal will, he is dropped into political oblivion with little fuss or bother since he no longer has a political party which serves as an independent source of political support able to take his case to the people. Indeed, the procedure of appealing to the people on a political issue is contrary to the basic premise of the 1962 constitutional system, which assumes that the interests of the King, the government, and the people are indivisible and identical.

POLITICAL DEVELOPMENT AND NATION BUILDING

The process of nation building is one of the most crucial questions facing most of the newly emerging Asian states, as it is also for those of Africa. At this stage interest is necessarily centered on the development of political institutions capable of achieving this basic goal. There would seem to be at teast three basic prerequisites in any country, no matter how developed or underdeveloped, for the effective implementation of nation-building programmes. These are:

(*a*) rationalization of the political process in conformity with the circumstances, needs, and history of the country;

(*b*) rationalization of the problem-solving administrative machinery; and

(*c*) a sense of national unity and solidarity.

The success or failure of political development in any country can be judged by its capacity to establish these prerequisites on an enduring basis.

From 1951 to 1960 the political process in Nepal sought

various forms of rationalization, the most important being the 1959 Constitution. But this was marked by such a resurgence of political irrationality and emotionalism that the 1959 rationalization of the political process was abruptly aborted in December, 1960. The new rationalization of the political process under the 1962 Constitution may be politically viable, but it has yet to demonstrate the capacity to achieve a rational, task-oriented, and predictable political process. Political tensions nnd dissidence resulting from the December, 1960, *coup* continue unresolved and perhaps are unresolvable withih the confines of the panchayat form of limited democracy. Aware of this undercurrent of hostility, the new government has assumed a posture of rigidity, denying both the need and the possibility of a compromise with its political critics. Since the opposition includes a significant proportion of the new political elites whose support is essential for the successful introduction of innovations in all spheres—political, economic, and social—the present regime finds itself in a basic dilemma. King Mahendra's ability to manipulate and use the traditional elites for his own purposes provides some degree of immediate political stability, but it is probably an obstruction to political development and the rationalization of the political process upon which long-term stability must be based.

The tentative nature of the political experiments carried out since 1951 had highly adverse effects, by thwarting the establishment of a rational, problem-solving administrative machinery. In addition to the unavoidable lack of technical skills and competence, the most serious obstacle to genuine administrative reorganization has been the low morale and insecurity of tenure of the new administrative elite. Almost every government since 1951 has gone through the ritual of "administrative reorganization" at least once during its period in office, but this was usually nothing more than a euphemism for the process of removing the political appointees of the previous regime and appointing its own candidates to these positions. This unhealthy administrative tradition has continued as a normal practice even after December, 1960, obstructing the rationalization of the administrative machinery. The lack of a sound, continuous, merit-based administrative system is probably the greatest single hindrance to the modernization and development of Nepal.

Perhaps the most frustrated and demoralized of the new administrative elites in Nepal are the technicians—engineers, doctors, scientists, and other specialists—who have often spent years in India and the West obtaining the requisite training for their vocations. In a country with a population of nearly ten million, there are only about a hundred and fifty engineers, two hundred doctors, a dozen scientists, and another dozen specialists in other fields. Instead of being valued for their specialized skills, they are often treated with contumely by the politically appointed administrators and even more so by the administrators' transient political bosses. In such a situation the technical elites often find in necessary to devote attention primarily to the complicated and fascinating game of intra-Secretariat politics, to the detriment of contributions in their fields of specialization. Without the proper recognition and utilization of the technical elites, however, it is inconceivable that any of the programmes for the modernization and industrialization of Nepal can achieve any substantial success except for the few essentially symbolic industrial projects established by the various foreign aid programmes.

It is, thus, only in the sphere of the third prerequisite for the modernization of Nepal—the development of a sense of nationhood—that there has been some remarkable progress since 1951, Nepali politics has pursued a self-consciously nationalistic policy since the overthrow of the Rana regime. This sense of Nepali nationalism is still largely confined to the people of central Nepal, but there are indications that it is spreading to the remoter hill areas to the east and west of Kathmandu and even to the Terai under the avowedly nationalistic goals of the present regime. The development of transportation and communication facilities, the continuing expansion of educational facilities, and the dominant political role assumed by the Crown may help to unify the country in the psychological as well as the political sense. The crucial question that remains to be answered is whether this still incipient sense of

Nepali nationalism can be mobilized for nation-building tasks, and if so under what conditions and at what political price. The early Shah rulers used it for territorial expansion and founded modern Nepal. The present ruler seems to view himself as the consolidator of the task started by his predecessors, but much of what he has attempted since ascending the throne is still programmatic. The panchayat innovation required more than five years of political incubation, and it will obviously require a longer time-span for testing in the world of realities.

2

Panchayat Democracy and its Form

What we have now is the issue of past. The future proceeds from the past and the present. In Nepal, the Panchayat democracy is the outcome of the practice of the parliamentary system and of the practical experience gained thereby. This democracy has come in as a novel political philosophy fulfilling a historic need. But the Panchayat system is not quite a new thing for us, the Nepalese. Our villages have been the foundations of our society and its economic position. The village Panchayat had been the medium in this direction for many centuries. The histories of many countries tell us that the village community is the most ancient form of the human social organization.

We come across proofs of the fact that even in different countries of Europe and Asia there were in ancient times those which we now call the village institutions. In our ancient texts like the "Mahabharata" and "Manusmriti" we have words like "gramasabha" and "gramasangha"—which immediately refer to such institutions. But their forms and functions were not similar to those of the institutions today. They were more important socially and economically than politically. In the modern democratic system of government the decentralisation of power is the basis of local self-government, and the local—

self government is the foundation of democracy. Therefore, the village Panchayat which is the chief stone in the foundation may be regarded as the real basis of democracy. The tendency of the Western countries embracing the modern democratic system, hints at the fact that the decentralisation of power is essential to the progress and prosperity of the individual and the society. The village Panchayat is such a factor in the social pattern as helps the cause and development of local self—government. In China which has got a long cultural background, the village community had been there in a well organized form, and it had been there since the very ancient times. During the period stretching between 1100 and 300 B.C. social pattern in China was divided into Kei, Li, Leh and Siang. This tribal organisation was in many respects akin to the organization in ancient Greece. In ancient Greece too the tribal organization was divided into Jen, Fartri and Tribe. The Chinese people living in village communities during that long period of three hundred years managed their governmental affairs by themselves. The saw, "the heaven is far above and the sovereign far out" was very popular among the commoners. According to Lin Yutang, the real government of China may be called the village imperialism. The principal organ of the village government was the council of patriarchs (elders) or managers. The head of the council was called Ti—Pao. The main functions of the council were to manage lights for the streets, to construct dykes and repair them, to erect walls, to superintend the marts, to build temples and mend them, to clean wells, to collect taxes, to settle disputes, and so on. Ninety five per cent of the disputes were settled by this very council. Self—government began in Asia earlier than in Europe. It began in the Greek city—states in 3 B.C. It seems to have been there also in the Roman city—states. It functioned, above all, as a religious institution. In the 13th century, self—government appeared in a developed form in the Alpine regions of Switzerland. It is believed that it developed in other countries of Europe only after it had developed in Switzerland.

In the Vedas we have the word "Gramini" which literally means 'the leader of the village'. In the Jataka tales occur two words "Gramasabha" and "shreni". Gramasabha may well be translated as "the village Panchayat' and 'shreni' as a 'trade union'. In the "Ramayana" by the great sage Valmiki as also in the "Arthashastra" by Kautilya, there are discussions on self—government institutions. Megasthenes, Huen—Tsang and Fahian have fully dwelt on the self—governing bodies in the cities and villages of India. In the "Neetishastra" of Shukracharya written in 7th century, there occure two words, 'gana' and 'paga'. Gana is perhaps the village Panchayat and 'paga' the town municipal corporation. Thus, we see that our self—governing bodies have come to us through several centuries. They had fully developed even when Europe was yet on the threshold of civilization.

In Britain, there are some traditional self—government institutions which had their origin during the Norman period of even prior to that. The Parish, there is the oldest in the field of self—government. It was, at first, invested with a religious purpose and continued to function as a religious institution till many days before the Norman conquest. In ancient times the inhabitants of a British Parish used to meet in the vestry to deliberate on matters concerned with the church.

In Britain, the Parish continued to exist as a unit of the church, even after, the decline of the feudal system. King Henry VIII suppressed and nearly abolished the monasteries, which led to the creation of problems regarding self—government. The government under Queen Elizabeth 1st discarded the monastery and embraced the Parish instead. It was in this way that the Parish ceased to function as a religious institution and switched itself over to the range of local self—Government. As a local unit, the County is perhaps older even than the Parish. Institutions of this kind existed there also in Greece, Rome, Switzerland and many other countries of Europe.

This system of local self—government institutions advanced and advanced with it the social, economic and political conditions of the people. The result was that changes Crept into this system. It evolved along with the gradual growth in the awakening and consciousness of the mass, and, therefore, side by side with the development of the modern democratic tradition the importance of its utility has increased too.

The decentralization of power has been an important aspect of the democratic tendency of the present century, and the assumption that the more the decentralization of power is greater is the success of democracy has been gaining ground. The mode in which Great Britain is governed to day is the result of the development that took place between 1832 and 1932 A.D. Local self government had been deemed specially important, during that period. The success achieved in the governmental functioning in Britain to day is, to a large extent the outcome of the success achieved by the local self—governing bodies there.

The principle of self—government does not fall under the rule of any imaginary or idealistic trend of thought, but its utiiity depends upon experience and living principle. In Britain where the successful system of self—government was founded at no definite time, it evolved along with gradual growth in the awakening and consciousness of the man. The present form of local self—government there is the result of the long process in the development through several centuries. Thus in Britain and other countries the local self—governing institutions have evolved alongside of the first school of civic life, so is local self—government accounted the first school or root of democracy. It is here that a citizen learns the A.B.C. of democracy.

The number of the functions of the state is growing day by day. In the 20th century the state has got many more functions. They are such as had not even been called into their imagination by the people of the 19th century. Local self government is very essential to smalling the number of functions of the central government; and, at the same time, the successful working of democracy depends upon the expertise of the people in practical politics. Local self-government educates the people in practical politics. It is for this reason that today, especially after the world war II, it is accounted more serviceable and momentous. Since it is the main pillar of local self—govern ment, the village Panchayat may be called the real foundation,- to be more exact the very life—of democracy. In India where the parliamentary system has been adopted, much emphasis is laid for the success of democracy on the development and advancement of the village Panchayats and the Panchayat Raj is regarded as the ideal of the democratic system.

The village Panchayat is a rural institution based on general co-operation. The village community founded on this kind of co-operation is to be found in even the human society of those times when man was busy shaking off barbarism and stepping into civilization. Even in the pre-historic age, or in the first stage of civilization, man lived in communities. As a matter of fact, the very community—life continuously led man ahead in the path of advancement and ultimately brought him to the social organisations as we have them today.

In the report submitted by the Village Panchayat Committee of the Congress Party of India at Delhi in 1954, it has been pointed out that in different countries of Europe and Asia the system of owning village institutions as local self-governing bodies was put to practice. Kropotkin, the distinguished Russian scholar, states in his book entitled "Mutual Aid" that in Europe fine co-operative life was lived in rural communities. According to the said report proofs have been found of the existence of ancient village institutions in Japan too. The works of M.D. Haxthausen and M. Tengo Borski show that the ancient village institution system continued to be in vogue in Russia even to the last century. Shree Jawahar Lal Nehru is of the opinion that the ancient Russian village institution system may well be compared with its counterpart in India. In Russia this ancient institution was called 'Mir'.

In India about 2300 years ago, local self—government had much flourished, during the reign of Chandra Gupta Maurya, and the village panchayat as a unit of it was well systematized. Same was the condition of the village Panchayat in the Middle ages. In this context, Prof. Sinha has got a reference to the statement of Mr. Raj Kamal Mukharjee which reads "Here the development of the independent local self—government was like the shell of a tortoise, under where lay natural concealed, and when there broke out a political storm, the culture of the country found itself safe and secure under it".

Towards the end of the 19th century, the salves in Serbia, Crotia and Austrian Slavonia had strong village fellow feeling. According to Heslar, such co-operative economic units were there also amongst the Germans. Till the time of the French Revolution, such institutions were known as 'parkonaries'. They were, in fact, the different forms of self-government, even though they differed in their forms and importance, from their counterparts to-day. The difference was, however, pointed out in the afore-said report of the Village Panchayat Committee of the Indian Congress.

According to a noted historian, traces have been discovered of the practice the Panchayat tradition also in the 6th century Nepal. In the opinion of another writer of history, the Panchayat system might have been gradually modified in name, form and function in the various ages it flourished in. But, in the Nepal, panchayat tradition is something very old. It has been an integral part of the social, religious and economic lives of the people of Nepal. In support of statement we can refer to the stone inscriptions as well as the social customs and practices that are still alive. In the time of Amsuvarma, every village was, in fact, governed by the 'pahancho', a group of five gentlemen. Likewise, about 55 'Vikram Sambat', the charge of maintaining peace in and looking after the security of the village were entrusted to the 'Astakula' or a body of eight representatives from eight different families in the village. The Astakula should also see whether justice was properly administered to the villages wanting it. A scholar of history discovered the word 'panchali' in an inscription at Chyasal Tole in Panta. It is such a word, he says, as can not he found anywhere outside the Nepalese inscriptions. Another compares the word 'panchali' with the word 'pancha' now current. Anyway, it is clear from the instances available that in Nepal, the panchayat is not a thing imposed of late lent a national tradition. Now, since it has come in as a political philosophy turned out a subject of research and investigation.

The 'word' Panchayat 'literally means a group of five person that meet and solve the local problems by themselves. According to a writer it is probable that in ancient times when counting by arithmetical figures was closely limited, people derived the knowledge of five 'from the five terminal members of the hand as also from the existence of the 'pancha mahabhoota' or the five great elements in the external world. People, therefore, would not have found it difficult to count up to five. The Roman figures are still written in a pentamerous system. This system was, to be sure, adopted from still older system. Therefore it is lent natural that 'five', the last figure in counting then, should be so important for the ancient man.

Consequently, the decision made by so big a moat of five to be accepted as final. In accordance with that tradition, anyone of the persons pronouncing the decision started being called a 'Pancha'. It was thus that the Panchayat came to be put to practice. It began to develop along with the developing social life.

'Kautilya has mentioned the existence of the republics of Vijjis (according to Dr. Regmi). This fact is further corroborated by the first Mandeva inscription which mentions about a war with the Mallas, who ruled beyond the Gandak river. Majjhim Nikaya, while dealing with the organisation of Budhist Sanghas, mentions about the Sanghas and Ganas of the above republic. "This is O' Goutama in respect of the Sangha Gana, for instance the Vijjis and Mallas". This proves the existence of powerful local institutions in Nepal even prior to the establishment of Lichavi Monarchy in Nepal".

Jayaswal has established that the Budha adopted the name as well as the constitution of the Budhist Sanghas from the political institution of Vijjis and Mallas, that is, from the soil of Nepal itself.

Prof. Upendra Narain Sinha has concluded in his thesis that "However the term PANCHALI (the earlier name of our Panchayat) has been for the first time used by the Lichavis of Nepal".

'At the same time it is worth nothing that the term Panchali has not been mentioned anywhere in the Indian inscriptions of Lichavis found at Basara (or Vaishali).

'A detailed study of the organisation of Lichavi Panchayat system throws more light in the antiquity of this institution in Nepal. Mahabharat clearly indicates that a powerful system of Panchayat existed in Nepal earlier in the name of Ganas and Sanghas which the Lichavis adopted both in spirit as well as from in the name of PANCHALI'.

Through the general survey of Lichavi inscriptions Prof. U.N. Sinha opines that the four types of Panchayats during the Lichavi period were:

1. the ordinary village,
2. the fortified village,
3. the group of villages, and
4. the towns, and those Panchayat possessed judicial powers managed the religious temples, rest house, public parks and had powers vested in them for their administration.

They regulated markets, imposed taxes and sometimes levied extra—tolls for specific objects of public utility. "Therefore the Hindu Policy of Nepal by its very nature stood or liberal autonomy and self governments of groups and associations. It never stood for extreme centralisation or over governments during ancient period.

We also had a particular form of the Panchayat which neither know the control of the central laws nor was guided by them. Here we had five old experienced 'gentlemen' who met to seek solutions of the various problems of the village and matter of community welfare. This has led to the establishment of a tradition by which the decision of the panchas were accepted as final.

This particular form of the Panchayat gradually became part of the village culture. Thus, we see that the Panchayat as tradition among the Nepalese people, is symbolic of their culture.

Even the countries, embracing the Parliamentary system have found it necessary to recognise the panchayat, which is nearly a part of the tradition and culture of their peoples. As the basis of their political system without provisions for local self—governing bodies like panchayats, it is just like a house without a foundation. No political system whose principle is to work contrarily to the tradition and culture of the people can remain stable democratically. In Nepal, the panchayat philosophy introduced by the king is but an expression of the tradition and culture of the Nepalese people in the form of a political philosophy.

Even before it set in as a political philosophy, the Panchayat had been constitutionally instituted for the first time in the history of Nepal, at Dang Deokhuri by the Sanad' of Baishakh 27, 1983. It was entitled Manyajana Kachahari, (an assembly of the superiors), and its members were electees of the local inhabitants. Local works concerning the settlement of minor disputes, as far as possible effecting compromise between the two contending parties and thereby relieving them of the trouble of transferring their cases to the law courts, and the safeguard of the properties of the people within the Panchayat area were all entrusted to it. Later, in 1987, Panchayats were started in the Kathmandu valley too. Consequently, there appeared nine Panchayats in Kathmandu, five in Latitpur and many in Bhaktapur. The practice of Panchayat was found to prove very beneficial. Therefore, in 1993, it was extended in many other parts of the country. Consequently Panchayats were started in Saptary, Bethary in the Terai and in west No. 2 and 3 in the hill regions. Each big 'Mauja' or a 'Mauja' composed of four to five villages came to own a separate

Panchayat. Each village Panchayat consisted of eight panchas, one of them nominated by the government and the remaining seven elected by the villagers themselves.

Later, the people were found to have developed an inclination to harvesting benefits from this village Panchayat tradition. Therefore, in 2006, a constitutional committee was formed, whose main function was to frame a code driving harmony into the form and functions of all the village Panchayats in the country. The constitutional committee enforced the Village Panchayat Act, 2006 and the Panchayat Judiciary Act, 2006, which enforced the village Panchayat to hold a fund of Rs. 100- in maximum for minor works of construction and management, and to try and settle law—suits. It was privileged to impose on one a fine amounting up to Rs. 25-or jail one for three months to the utmost.

After the introduction of democracy into the country, the government of Nepal aimed at making the Panchayat system still more pervading. In the years 2008, 2009, 2010, and 2013 Panchayat officers were sent to different areas of the country, and as many as 826 Panchayats came to be instituted. But, keeping in view gradual inscrease in the demand for more Panchayats in the country, the government annulled the Village Panchayat Act, 2006, and the Panchayat Judiciary Act, 2006, and brought into effect the Village Panchayat Act, 2013. Special attention was paid in this new act on bettering the Panchayat system and on construction works so essential to the development of the country. The Act did not invest judicial powers on the village Panchayats; but according to clause no, 44 of the Act, the government could, by a special order, entitle all or some of the village Panchayats in the entire kingdom to exercise the powers exercised by the regional court of law. Finding that mere enforcement of the Act would pay little, the government, in the begining of the year 2014, divided the entire kingdom into sixteen zones. Each zone got a Panchayat zone inspector. Now, provision were made for the appointments of 57 sub—inspectors, 265 samyojaks (co—ordinators), 16 junior clerks, and 13 peons for one years, and 328 sahakari (co—operators), and 656 peons for four months. Later, certain modifications were made in the appointments whereby all except some of the co-ordinators to be appointed for one year, came to be appointed. They were sent to different districts, and some Panchayats were created in 2014 too. But the government decided on annulling this system so as to ensure a still better one, and consequently, they were all dismissed in Kartik, 2014.

In 2016, however, it was decided that as many as 33 panchayat offices set up in the entire country—32 in the districts and one in the valley. Provisions were accordingly made for the appointment in total of 274 staff members: 33 panchayat officers, 33 junior clerks, 99 peons and 109 panchayat supervisors. Each panchayat office, thus, got one panchayat officer, one junior clerk and 3 peons. Each panchayat supervisor was appointed with reference to each of the 109 parliamentary electoral units. All of the afore—said members of the panchayat office staffs were appointed for the period ending in the completion of the work of organizing and re-organizing the panchayats. The 33 panchayat officers and the 109 panchayat supervisors were appointed and trained in panchayat affairs at Lal Darbar. Later, since Nepal came to be divided into 14 zones and 75 development districts under the panchayat democratic system, the panchayat officers and the supervisors appointed with reference to the 109 parliamentary electoral units naturally dismissed. Then, in 2018, provisions were made for the appoinment of 14 panchayat officers and 75 panchayat supervisors. Each Zone, thus, got a panchayat officer and a panchayat supervisor. Arrangements were made for training the panchayat officers and supervisors at the Rural Development Institution at Jawalakhel, Kathmandu.

Besides the panchayat officers and supervisors, there were appointed 56 personnel for each zone. Thus, each zone got one 'bahidar', one 'mukhia', and 2 peons, and each development district one 'bahidar' and one peon. In this way the total number of the staff—members appointed came to be 295. These 295 panchayat personnel organised as many as 3646 village panchayats throughout Nepal. The village panchayats together did form the lowest level in the panchayat democratic system.

The village panchayats are represented in the district panchayats concerned. It is in this process that the representatives of the village people go, through the second and third levels of the panchayat, to the highest level—the National Panchayat, the supreme institution represented by the entire population of the country.

Thus, through a long experience of fruitful consequences, the panchayat has been so much integrated with the life of the people even the governments that came previous to 2017 could not disregard it. Even the Rana regime had not ignored it as a system.

On the 7th of Falgun. 1975 (during the rule of the Rana prime minister, Chandra Shamshera), Keshar Sing Gurung had put forward that in order to improve the administrative machinery in a democratic way a small fraction of the governing power should be entrusted to the representatives of the people. The suggestion was, however, taken into consideration, and by way of showing that people had been granted the right of local self—government, an election was ordained to be held in Paush, 1976, for the organization of the city municipality, one of the principal institutions in the system of local self—government. Thus, in the 2nd of Paush, 1976, the city municipality, very much similar to an elected unit in the modern democratic system, was for the first time instituted. Even through there was no democratic system of government in Nepal then, yet the institution of the city municipality may, although indirectly, be regarded as the commencement of local self—government.

The city of Kathmandu was divided into two halves—the upper half and the lower half; and a 'hakim' was appointed for each half. Besides the 'hakims', there were the chairman, the Vice—chairman, some government employees and nine members elected by the townsmen. Thus both the 'hakims' and those in the municipality were jointly given the charge of minicipality affairs. Among nine members, referred to above, 4 were elected from the Bhotahity side and the remaining 5 from other parts of the city. In this election, city—dwellers at the age of twenty or above were entitled to exercise their franchise.

In 1979, an effort was made to make the city municipality more regular in its working and more capable of big ventures. It was, therefore, specially authorized to expend Rs. 50,000 more every year. In 1979, oversears and engineers were appointed to help it in all its technological attempts. A special provision was made whereby old codes concerning it were annulled and new codes enforced.

The entire working of the Kathmandu Municipality was entrusted to two different sectors. But, later, when it grew in bulk, the number of sector was raised to five. The importance of the municipality had been fully realised, an election for the Kathmandu Municipality was held in Ashadha, 2004. Thus, the Kathmandu Municipality came to be composed of 31 members, 21 of them elected by the populace and 10 nominated by the government. It may, however, be noted that the chairman of the Kathmandu Municpality was one of the members appointed by the government and the vice—chairman one of those elected by the people. For this election, the whole of the Kathmandu Municipality area was divided into 21 election units called Blocks. Ever since the Kathmandu area has got 21 blocks. In 2010, another election for the Kathmandu Municipality was held, the townsmen could elect only 18 of the many candidates, although the number of blocks figuered 21.

In 2010, there came the Municipal Act, 2009. The Act was designed to the democratic system of government; and, accordingly, an election for the Municipality was held in the month of Bhadra, 2010. According to this Act, any specific area, of any strength of population or with its total income amounting to any figure, could own a municipality, provided its people placed a demand for or the government deemed it necessary to provide it with one as circumstances suggested. Besides Kathmandu, Lalitpur and Bhaktapur, cities like Bhadrapur (Jhapa), Biratnagar, Birganj, Palpa, Tansen came to own municipalities.

It cannot, however, be affirmed that these institutions were very much similar to the organs of the modern demoeratic system, yet it may be called that they resembled them to a certain extent. The Rana regime then had, however, realized the desire of the people for self—government, and in order to meet this desire had sanctioned the organizations of self—governing bodies. These self—governing institutions may well be called the primal forms of the city Panchayats to—day. After the implementation of the Panchayat system Nagar Panchayat Ain (Aet) 2019, was published. And "realising that only decentralisation programme can bring an all round development of the country, and this policy of decentralisation can be strengthened only by the Panchayat system. Like in village, in cities also City Panchayats have been established, and these Panchayats are provided with economic, social and cultural assistance according to their need in order to facilitate people for maximum participation in administration." All municipalities formed under the Nagarpalika, Ain (Act) 2009 have been changed into Nagar Panchayats. Apart from this the Nagar Panchayat Ain 2009 with all its amendments and the rules of Nagar Palika elections published in Nepal gazette in 2010 have been terminated.

In the Nagar panchayat Ain, all City Panchayats are allowed certain rights and duties. This Nagar Panchayat Ain is quite in accordance with the system of government. These Nagar Panchayats are not only the fundamental institutions but also are taken as important basic institutions of the National politics. According to the provision of this Act one—third of the total elected members of the City Panchayats reaches at the District Assembly, from District Assembly to District Panchayat, from District Panchayat to Zonal Assembly and lastly to the Rastria Panchayat. And only the member of the Rastriya Panchayat can be a minister. Thus members of a City Panchayat through stages can reach to the government.

Thus, for Nepal, the Panchayat tradition is ancient as anything and representative of her culture. The main ideal of the decentralization of power is to make the self-governing bodies the real bases of democracy as far as possible. This is why the democratic system which issues from the Panchayats, the principal pillars of self—government, may be called real and basic democracy, or building democracy from the roots.

It is worth while to dwell here on the characteristic factors that determine the organizational forms of the Panchayat system. The following is a list of the factors:

(*a*) Adult franchise

(*b*) well—developed people's representative system.

(*c*) The principle of common good.

(*d*) Maximum decentralization of administration based on national unity.

It may, however, be noted that the above characteristic factors constitute the basis of any democratic system of the world.

The entire organisation of the Nepalese Panchayat system is put at two different levels:

1. the local panchayats, and
2. the National Panchayat

By the local Panchayats here we mean;

1. the village or city Panchayats
2. the District Panchayats
3. the Anchal (Zonal) sabha.

There is a National Panchayat in the centre. This is the supreme representative body in the country and highest level of the system. Thus it is called a four—tier Panchayat system.

Village Panchayat: Gaun Shabha is the lowest and basic tier of the Panchayat system. This is a village assembly. The area of a village or a group of villages is called Gaun Shabha as declared by the government on careful consideration of its geographical location, population and transportation facilities etc. Generally the area of gaun shabha comprises a population proportionately 2500. This gaun shabha is a corporate body.

All persons who have attained the age of twenty one and are living within the area of its jurisdiction are regarded the members of the gaun shabha. But those persons cannot be the members who are not the Nepalese citizen and are insane.

Every gaun shabha elects an executive body which is called 'Gaun Panchayat' (village Panchayat). In the first election the members of the gaun panchayat were nine and Pradhan and Upa—Pradhan Pancha were elected by the panchayat members among themselves. But now, according to the fourth amendment, 2022 of the Village Panchayat Act the numbers of the village panchayat members increased upto eleven including Pradhan and Upapradhan Panchas. And the Pradhan and Upa—pradhan Panchas are to be elected directly by the gaun shabha. Their election is to be held by secret ballot. But no one can be elected Pradhan and Upapradhan Panchas without getting fifty per cent of casted votes. Pradhan and Upapradhan Panchas are ex--officio chairman and vice chairman of the Gaun shabha.

For the election of a village panchayat every gaun shabha is divided into nine wards and from every ward one representative is elected for the village Panchayat by members of the ward.

Among the members of the village panchayat one third (three) retire every two years and in their place new members are elected. Thus the village Panchayat is a continous body.

The tenure of office of the members is six years. But in the first election of panchayat members the tenure of office of one third was of two years, of another one third was of four years and of the remaining one third was of six years. This question of the tenure of office was decided by the Pradhan Pancha by casting lots.

The Pradan Pancha, the Upa—Pradhan Pancha or any member can be removed from their office even before the completion of their tenure on the following grounds:

1. If the District Panchayat decides them of bad character and unable to discharge their duties and District Assembly passess a resolution, in a general meeting, by a simple majority to remove them from their office.
2. In the case of Pradhan and Upa—Pradhan Pancha if the two—third majority of the members of the gaun Shabha passes the resolution to remove them.
3. In the case of other members of Gaun Panchayat if the resolution to remove is passed by a two—third majority of the members of the ward present and voting in the meeting.

Following persons are not eligible for the membership of the village panchayat:

1. those who are not the members of Gaun Shabha.
2. Government servants.
3. employees of the Gaun Shabha.
4. Defaulters to the Gaun Shabha.
5. Bankrupts.
6. Proved immoral from the court.
7. those who sue against the Gaun Shabha and become absent, without any proper reason, continuously in the three meetings of Gaun Shabha.

Pradhan Pancha, Upa Pradhan Pancha or other members of village Panchayat can submit resignation from the membership of Panchayat.

Duties of the Village Panchayat: Village Panchayat, under the general supervision of District Panchayat performs the following duties:

1. the construction and maintenance of roads and bridges within the Panchayat area.
2. Plantation of trees on both sides of the road.
3. To make necessary arraugements for checking the spread of infections disease.
4. To run primary schools for the education of the children of the village.
5. Construction and maintenance of well, ponds, dam, canals etc.
6. To start cottage industries and to make them popular.
7. To promote cooperatives.
8. To help the work done by the government for public good and popularise them.
9. To help the work of development started by District Panchayat or the District development committee.
10. To make measures for increasing agricultural production by scientific method, provision of better seeds, fertilizers, better instruments etc.
11. To make sanitary arragement and to make them popular.

Thus the Village Panchayat undertakes small development works of village level which can be accomplished with their own resources and labour. Big projects and such works which benefit more than one village Panchayats are performed by higher levels.

The Village Panchayats are given some economic rights because it needs "funds" to perform its duties. Therefore, Village Panchayats are given the right to levy certain taxes within their area of jurisdiction, with approval of Gaun Shabha.

Every Gaun Shabha has its own "village fund". All the sums collected from the taxes levied by the Gaun Shabha. Government's grant, income from moveable and immoveable property, gift and donations etc. are deposited in the Village fund. Necessary arrangements for the maintenance of fund and keeping of its aecount is made by the Gaun Shabha. And the general administration of the village fund is carried on by the village Panchayat. Every year Village Panchayat must present its estimated budget for that year in the meeting of the Gaun Shabha. Village Panchayat spends in accordance with the budget and plan approved by the Gaun Shabha.

Arrangement has been made in the Act for cheeking the accounts of the Village Panchayat, His Majesty Government also can cheek the accounts.

Political Rights: Among the four tiers of the system Village Panchayat is regarded as basic organisation of local self government and decentralisation of powers. Alongside it also has been regarded as the basic political unit. A member of this basic unit reaches in the centre, through the higher levels, by a filtering process. Therefore, the panchayat takes part in the national politics. The Village Panchayat can send its representative in the government. This is the significant political rights. Thus the Village Panchayat enjoys political right. Village Panchayat inspires the people to take part in day—to—day administration, keeps them vigilant and thus exercises its political right into practice. The right to send a representative in the government is regarded very important political right in the democratic age of today.

Judicial Powers: Village Panchayat are given certain judicial powers also. The main reason for this is to avoid unnecessary expenses and travelling long distances to the court for minor cases. According to the provision of the Act Village Panchayat can decide such minor cases in the Panchayat itself. Village Panchayat can make both the contending parties agree for compromise under the provision of the prevailing Act of the land. Village problems and mutual dissentions of the village can be well understood by the villagers themselves. This is why the

Village Panchayats are given the right to decide the minor cases.

In order to keep records of important papers and account. Village Panchayat can appoint a 'Gaun Sevaka' and if necessary others as well. This 'Gaun Sevaka' also acts as a Secretary. After the fourth amendment of 2022 in the village Panchayat Act there is a provision for the Pradhan Pancha to have remuneration.

The general meeting of the Gaun Sabha must be at least twice a year—after the winter harvest and after the summer harvest. The meeting of both the Village Panchayat and the Gaun Sabha is presided over by the Pradhan Pancha.

According to the fourth amendment of 2022 ten per cent of the members of Gaun Sabha showing reasonable cause demands for meeting addressed to the chairman and in the absence of Pradhan Pancha to the Upa—Pradhan Pancha or if the Gaun Panchayat decides to call such meeting, special meeting is called. In the absence of chairman and vice—chairman the eldest member of Gaun Sabha should be addressed for calling such meeting. Prior to this amendment 20 per cent of the members of Gaun Sabha was required for such meeting.

For the quorum of the general meeting of Gaun Sabha at least ten per cent, and for the special meeting (or extra ordinary) at least 20 per cent of the total membership is required.

Nagara (*City*) *Panchayat*: Like the Gaun Panchayat in the rural area the city Panchayat has been established in the city area. In a city consisting of ten thousands or more than that population H.M.G. can establish a city Panchayat. Any person residing within the area of Nagara Panchayat generally upto the one year, or who has a home within the area or a commercial business and who has any immoveable property within the area, and who has attained the age of 21 in the year when the election of the members of Nagara Panchayat takes place, has the right to vote in the Nagara Panchayat election. But the following persons are not given the right to vote:

1. Non Nepali Citizen,
2. Insanes.

Government servants, proved immorals, defaulters to the Nagara Panchayat, bankrupts those who have been punished for any misconduct in the election of Nagara Panchayat and those who are illiterate are not eligible for the membership of the Nagara Panchayat. According to the population of city the membership of the city Panchayat can be nine in the minimum and thirty three in the maximum. These members are elected by secret ballots. If H.M.G. thinks necessary it can nominate any proper person in Nagara Panchayat. But the number of such nominated persons should not exceed one fourth of the number of the elected members. The nominated member should not be eligiblefor the membership of District Panchayat. After the election of the city Panchayat the members of the city Panchayat elect the Pradhan Pancha and Upa—Pradhan Pancha among themselves, and they must be elected by the two—third majority of the total members.

The tenure of office of the members is six years. But Pradhan Pancha and Upa-Pradhan Pancha are elected only for two years.

Nagara panchayat is a continuous and corporate body.

The general meeting of the Nagara Panchayat must be held once in a month. But if at least one third of the members of Nagara Panchayat demand in writing for calling the meeting of Nagara Panchayat the chairman has to call the meeting within 7 days.

No meeting should be held without the quorum of at least one third members of Nagara Panchayat.

The budget of Nagara Panchayat can be discussed and accepted only in that meeting in which at least fifty per cent of the members are present. If the members will not present up to the required quorum continuously for three meetings the fourth meeting can be held whatsoever the number of the members may be present.

The Nagara Panchayat, subject to the law can undertake all tasks for the progress of the city and the good of the people. Nagara Panchayat performs the following important functions.

1. Construction and maintenance of roads, bridges culverts and inns.
2. To make arrangement for drinking water.
3. To destroy things which harm public health, and to improve health service.
4. To make arrangement for the prevention of the disease.
5. To keep records of houses and lands within the area.
6. To restrict immoral and dangerous business.
7. To co-operate in the work started by District Panchayat or district development committee.

Nagara Panchayat can undertake all tasks necessary for public welfare; like arrangement of light on the roads, construction and establishment of dispenseries. plantation of trees on both sides of the road and arrangement for fairs and exhibition etc.

There has been provision of Nagara Panchayat fund. The sums of taxes levied by Nagara Panchayat rents, grant and donation received by Nagara Panchayat, income from the moveable or immoveable property of Nagara Panchayat are collected in this fund.

The accounts of Nagara Panchayat can be checked on the recommendation of Nagara Panchayat or by the person directly appointed by the H.M.G. No new building can be erected without the permission of Nagara Panchayat within its area. At present there are 14 Nagara Panchayats in the country.

The Nagara Panchayat is but a modified name of the municipality which was recognised, even during the period when Nepal practised the parliamentary system, as a chief organ of Local self government. The municipality is renamed the 'Nagara Panchayat' in order to drive home uniformity in system of local self-government under the panchayat system. Its members, elected as the representatives by the Nagara Panchayat, are taken in also as members to the District Panchayat concerned. This shows an attempt behind it at making the entire self—government system, a systematic chain process.

District Panchayat: The second tier of the Panchayat system is "Jilla Sabha" (district assembly). This is composed of the representatives elected by both the 'Gaun panchayat' and the Nagara Panchayat. This jilla sabha elects an executive body called Jilla Panchayat' (district panchayat). This is on the district level.

The main objective of this level is to guide and to co-ordinate the works of village and Nagara Panchayats. It initiates also the works of district level. The development districts are regarded the jurisdiction of district panchayats. There are 75 district panchayats on the basis of the development blocks in the country.

Jilla Sabha comprises of one representative from every Village Panchayat elected from among its members and one third of the total elected members of the Nagara Panchayat.

This jilla sabha is a continuous, corporate and autonomous body. Nobody is eligible for the membership of more than one jilla sabha at one time.

Those, who are insanes or dumb, proved immoral, bankrupts, government servants and employees of jilla Sabha, are not eligible to be elected for the membership and to retain the membership of jilla sabha. The member of the jilla sabha is ineligible to continue his membership on the following conditions:

1. if he becomes a share—holder directly or indirectly in the contract concerning the district panchayat of which he is member;
2. if he takes part in the sue against the district panchayat of which he is a member;
3. if the place where he resides is declared as outside the area of the Jilla Sabha;
4. without any reasonable cause if he becomes absent continuously from three meetings of Jilla Sabha and;
5. if he does not reside generally within the area of Jilla Sabha.

The meeting of the District Assembly (Jilla Sabha) must be held two times a year—one after the summer harvest and the other after the winter harvest. In between the two meetings more than six months should not elapse. For the quorum of the meeting of Jilla Sabha at least fifty per cent of the members must present. If the required number does not meet at first meeting and next meeting is called only thirty five per cent of the members will make proceeding possible.

Generally meeting of the Jilla Sabha is summoned in accordance with the decision of the District Panchayat. If 20 per cent of the members of the Jilla Sabha, showing reasonable cause, asks for discussion on any particular subject the Chairman will have to call the meeting within 3 days.

Jilla Sabha (District Assembly) elects an executive committee of eleven members including one chairman; one vice chairman and nine other members. First of all, the chairman and the vice chairman are elected and the other nine members are elected later on.

The tenure of office of the chairman and the vice chairman

will be of two years and that of other nine members will of six years. In the first election the tenure of one third members was of two years, of another one third four years and of the remaining one third six years. Thus the District Panchayat is a continuous body. Three members of it retire in every two year and new members will be elected in their places.

For a meeting of the District Panchayat more than half of its members must be present. The budget of the District Panchayat must be accepted by a majority of at least 50 per cent of its members.

The chairman and the vice—chairman or other members of the District Panchayat can submit the resignation and retire from their office. They can also be removed by a vote of no—confidence passed by two third majority of the total members of Distrct Assembly.

Jilla Sabha performs functions of inspection of the details of income and expenditure prepared by the District Panchayat. It also discusses progress report submitted by the District Panchayat, and discusses the budget and development-plans submitted by the District Panchayat, plans to levy taxes subscribtions etc., within the rights given by law.

Jilla Panchayat performs the following important functions:

1. To make arrangements for primary and secondary education in accordance with the policy and rules of H.M.G.
2. To initiate the work for agricultural development and livestock improvement.
3. To perform functions of public welfare such as: improvement in health service, construction and maintenance of roads, bridges, wells, ponds, dams, canals etc.
4. To make arrangement for irrigation at district level.
5. To initiate the spirit of co-operation.
6. To execute all the district level plans of H.M.G.

7. Supervison and inspection of village and city panchayats lying within the jurisdiction of the District Panchayat.
8. To make annual inspection and give necessary direction regarding income and expenditure of the village and city panchayats.
9. To perform works as directed by H.M.G.
10. To prepare the estimated budget of income and expenditure of the Jilla Panchayat and to submit it in the Jilla Sabha.
11. To levy fees on individuals who make use of library, inn. roads, bridge or ghats that are constructed or controlled by the District Panchayat.

The District Panchayat can delegate and hand over any of its authority or power to any committee or sub-committee, to chairman or vice—chairman, to its members or secretary. The chairman of District Panchayat can delegate his power to the secretary or to the vice—chairman or any member. Duties of a chairman is to summon the meeting of the District Panchayat, to preside over the meeting and to execute the plans approved by the District Panchayat. In the absence of chairman vice-chairman will perform his duties and will exercise his powers.

Every District Panchayat has one secretary. He works under the supervision of the chairman. To help his work H.M.G. can appoint an assistant secretary. The secretary will keep the record of the decision of the District Panchayat, execute the decisions under the general supervision of the chairman, will give necessary advice to the District Panchayat in matter of district development works and will perform the works entrusted to him by the Act. For every District Panchayat H.M.G. also has made arrangement for other regular staffs also to work in various fields. Other officials of district level also will work under the District Panchayat. The chairman, vice-chairman and other members will also receive remuneration from the treasury of Jilla Sabha.

Every District Assembly has its own fund. Aids given by H.M.G. and income from other sources of the District

Panchayat. the amount of taxes levied by the District Assembly, fees, income from moveable or immoveable property of District Assembly are deposited in this fund. This treasury is at the disposal of the secretary of the District Panchayat and he will spend the fund subject to the provision of the District Panchayat.

The accounts of the District Panchayat will be audited by an individual appointed by H.M.G. In order to assist the secretary, there will be other officials in the office of District Panchayat.

H.M.G. can inspect and see to it that works done by District Panchayat are in conformity with the laws and regulations. H.M.G. from the standpoint of public welfare can order the District Panchayat to do or not to do certain works. This is the special privilege of H.M.G.

H.M.G. can nominate the required number of members in the districts which have less than twenty village Panchayats and the membership of the District Assembly is less than twenty. Such nominated members will hold their office in accordance with the pleasure of His Majesty's Government. Their rights and duties will be similar to that of elected members.

In case a District Panchayat does not perform its duties regularly or misuses its powers, H.M.G. can suspend or dissolve it and hold another election.

Anchal Sabha: The third tier of Panchayat system is the Anchal Sabha (Zonal Assembly). This tier comprises of all members of the Jilla Panchayats of a Zone. The members of Zonal Assembly elect among themselves one chairman and vice-chairman. The tenure of office of the chairman and the vice-chairman will be of two years. This Anchal Sabha is an ever rolling and an autonomous body.

The insanes, proved immoral, bankrupts government servants, employees of Gaun Panchayat, Nagar Panchayat and

Jilla Sabha are not eligible for the membership of Anchal (Zonal) Sabha.

The Meeting of Anchal Sabha must be held two times in every year. But more than six months should not elapse in between the two meetings. The meeting of the Anchal Sabha is summoned by the chairman. For the quorum of the meeting 40 per cent of the total members of the Anchal Sabha must present. And 25 per cent of the members will meet the quorum for the second meeting if the first meeting was suspended for want of quorum.

The following persons can attend the conference of Anchal Sabha but they have no right to vote:

1. From the women's organisation of Zonal level. 3
2. From the Nepal Kishan Sangathan. 4
3. From the Youth Organisation. 4
4. From the Majadura sangathan. 2
5. From the organisation of Exmilitary men. 2
6. From the Graduates (nominated). 4

The Anchal Sabha and other Zonal officials may attend the Conference as observer but they will not have the right to vote.

If there is any complain about inability of any member of the Anchal Sabha the decision of the supreme court is regarded as final.

Every Anchal Sabha has its own treasury and this fund will be at the disposal of the secretary. He will spend the fund subject to the provisions and under the rules and regulations.

Anchal Sabha can share in the income of Jilla Panchayats within its area of jurisdiction to the extent of 10 per cent and can also levy certain taxes on the area benefiting from its special works.

Accounts of Anchal Sabha will be audited every year by an individual appointed by H.M.G.

Just like Jilla Panchayats H.M.G. can inspect and see to it that works done by the Anchal Sabha in Conformity with the laws and regulations and can order the Anchal Sabha to do or not to do certain acts in the interest of general welfare.

The police have to co-operate to execute decisions of all these three levels of Panchayat system.

Rastriya Panchayat: The highest and the fourth tier of the Panchayat system is the Rastriya Panchayat, whose experienced members do come leaving three tiers behind. Thus the nature of this House, its composition, and functions are as well defined by the constitution as the composition, functions and rights of village Panchayat, city panchayat and Zilla Panchayat and Anchal Sabha are defined by the Act. The Rastriya Panchayat is a permanent body and comprises of the representatives of the entire population. The Rastriya Panchayat has been composed in such a way that almost all important sections of society are represented in it. This kind of representation is the demand of the day. In the Rastriya Panchayat there are altogether 125 members.

1. Zonal Assemblies elect 90 members to the Rastriya Panchayat in such a way that at least one member is elected from each of the 75 development districts.
2. Different class organisations elect 15 members of the Rastriya Panchayat, In which;
   (*a*) Nepal Peasants Organisation elects 4 members.
   (*b*) Nepal Youth Organisation also elects 4 members.
   (*c*) Nepal Women's Organisation elects 3 members.
   (*d*) Nepal Ex-servicemen Organisation elects 2 members.
   (*e*) The Nepal Labour organisation elects—2 members.
3. Graduates elect 4 members out of themselves.
4. His Majesty nominates 15 per cent of the total representatives, i.e. 16 nominees.

Since the Rastriya Panchayat is composed of the members of working class, class organisation and graduates, the House is wider in representation.

To be a member of the Rastriya Panchayat one must be a citizen of Nepal and at least 25 years in age. Except ministers or assistant minister, candidate should not be servant of His Majesty's government. Similarly a candidate should not be ineligible by law and should not have been previously expelled from the Rastriya Panchayat on charge of breaking secrecy of the House.

Members are elected from Zonal Assemblies for the Rastriya panchayat for a period of six years and other members for a period of 4 years. But a provision has been made and according to which one third of the total members do retire in every two years. In the first election the tenure of the representatives was determined by lottery system. It is due to this reason that the Rastriya Panchayat is called a permanent or ever rolling body.

The Term of a member of the Rastriya Panchayat will expire if he resigns or lacks the above said qualifications or abstains himself from taking part in the meeting of the Rastriya Panchayat for more than a period of three months without due notice.

A member of the Rastriya Panchayat will be expelled from the House on the ground of revealing secrecy of the legislative body if a tribunal composed of a judge of the Supreme Court appointed by His Majesty and Chairman of the House and a person of State Council (who is not a member of the House) approves allegation and His Majesty accepts the same. The vacant seat will be filled by the same procedure under which the ex-member was elected or nominated as the case may be. If a seat is vacant for any one of the above mentioned reasons them election will be held or nomination be made for remaining period of the term only. Every member of the Rastriya Panchayat, before assuming his seat has to take an oath in on the way as His Majesty prescribes.

These procedures are almost identical even in parliamentary system of government. In parliamentary system all members of the House are elected at a time directly by the people. But in case of the Panchayat system, members of the Rastriya Panchayat are, although elected directly by the people at village level, reach the House by a filtering system.

Members of the Rastriya Panchayat are also members of village panchayats. Thus the Rastriya Panchayat is an institution which has been developed right from the village level. The chairman of the Rastriya Panchayat is elected by the members themselves which is subject to approval of His Majesty. The term of the Chairman of the Rastriya Panchayat is for two years but he is eligible for re-election. The term of the chairmen expires on the following conditions:

1. If he resigns.
2. If he no longer remains member of the Rastriya Panchayat.
3. If his term is over.
4. If two—third members of the House passes a vote of no-confidence and His Majesty approves the same.

If the Chairman of the House cannot discharge his duties on the ground of ill health or on any other ground then His Majesty assigns his duty to vice-chairman of the House.

Members of the Rastriya Panchayat elect one Vice-chairman. In the absence of the Chairman, the Vice-chairman conducts all his business. The term of office of the vice-chairman is also for a period of two years but he is eligible for re-election. If he submits resignation addressing the chairman of the Rastriya Panchayat, if he is no longer remains member of the House and if his term is over the post of Vice-chairman an remains vacant.

Steering Committee: There is a provision of a Steering Committee "consisting of twenty—one members to advise the chairman of the Rastriya Panchayat with regard to proper arrangement of business before the Rastriya Panchayat and also in other matters. Other functions of the steering Committee shall be in accordance with the provisions laid down in the rules of the Rastriya Panchayat.

"The Chairman and vice-chairman of the Rastriya Panchayat shall be the ex-officio chairman and Vice-Chairman. respectively of the Steering Committee, and the Prime Minister, Ministers for Finance, Home, Panchayat and Law shall be the ex-officio members thereof. Other members of Steering Committee shall be elected by the members of Rastriya Panchayat in the manner laid down in rules of Rastriya Panchayat" Except the ex-officio members of the steering committee the form of other members has been fixed for two years.

According to the Constitution His Majesty can summon and prorogue the session of the Rastriya Panchayat. But there should not elapse more than six months between the end of one session and the beginning of the other. His Majesty, if he thinks necessary to summon a meeting of the Rastriya Panchayat, may fix the date and time of such meeting at any time and the meeting shall be held on the date and time so fixed.

According to the constitution 'the proceedings of the Rastriya Panchayat or any of its committee shall not be held in open. But this does not mean that every thing is secret about the Rastriya Panchayat. Rastriaya Panchayat deals with public issues. Every member coming from the different parts of the country can take part in discussion there. No body can say this debate is secret when so many people's representatives take part in it. More over, the activities of the Rastriya Panchayat are made public through the means of mass communications, as radio and newspapers. All laws passed by the Rastriya Panchayat are duly published and government strictly follows it. Similarly the House passes the budget of the country. This no longer can be called a secret. In Parliamentary form of government the session of the House is open to all. But in that form of government any bill introduced by the majority party, although be possible in theory, can not be changed in practice. Because that can be passed easily without any change on the basis of brute majority. But most of the bills introduced in the Rastriya Panchayat have not been so far passed without any, may be a slightest, change. So there is no logic in the argument that the discussions of the Rastriya Panchayat are secret and one cannot get a chance to express his opinion there. So the word "secret" in this context means, "to save the Rastriya Panchayat from being the centre of individual propaganda of its members".

"Any person may observe a meeting on the occasion of address to the Rastriya Panchayat by His Majesty or by any distinguished invite if the chairman or the secretary of the Rastriya Panchayat gives permission". In this context it is worth recalling the saying of the ex-Chairman of the Rastriya Panchayat Mr. Rajeswar Devkota. He writes:

> "The secrecy of the Rastriya Panchayat is not a fundamental question, it is simply a side issue. Even if His Majesty puts to an end of this secrecy there will not come any basic change in the workings of the House. The only reason behind this is to run the whole show efficiently so that no member could try to attract attention of audience towards himself unnecessarily and more deeds could be accomplished in a shorter period of time. Since all follow same principles and are representatives of people it does matter very little as what do they say. The most important thing is what do they enact. There is no quarrel inside the Rastriya Panchayat regarding principles. The very reason behind this secrecy is to save time which otherwise would have been spent in baseless talks".

"The constitution has clearly mentioned all about privileges and duties of the Rastriya Panchayat. On the basis of the constitution itself the Rastriya Panchayat has its own rulings. Moreover the Rastriya Panchayat presents every detail about its activities to the people. In this way every proceeding of the Rastriya Panchayat is made public. His Majesty can send a message to the Rastriya Panchayat. In such a case the Rastriya

Panchayat has to present its own opinion regarding the contents of the message. The Rastriya Panchayat may, by a motion passed by a majority of the members, present an address to His Majesty.

Constitutionally 'no discussion shall take place in the Rastriya Panchayat with regard to the conduct of His Majesty, Her Majesty the Queen and the successors to the Throne" But this does not restrict the members to criticise the activities of His Majesty's Government. The Rastriya Panchayat can not discuss the conduct of a judge in the discharge of his duty. But the Rastriya Panchayat can present an address to His Majesty to form a commission consisting of a person or persons for finding out whether the chief justice or the judge as the case may be is unable to perform his duties due to incapacity or misbehaviour. 'No discussion can be held in the Rastriya Panchayat with respect to any matter relating to a case pending in any court in Nepal'.

Rastriya Panchayat has certain privileges also "Subject to the Provisions of the constitution and the rules of the Rastriya Panchayat, there shall be full freedom of speech in the Rastriya Panchayat and no member of the Rastriya Panchayat shall be arrested, taken into custody or be liable to proceedings in any court in respect of any thing said or any vote cast by him in the Rastriya Panchayat or any of its committees"

'The Rastriya Panchayat shall have full powers to regulate its internal matters and only the Rastriya Panchayat shall have authority to decide whether any proceedings of the Rastriya Panchayat is regular or otherwise and no question thereof shall be raised in any court. Therefore no court has the right to speak regarding the working of the Rastriya Panchayat.

No member of the Rastriya Panchayat shall be arrested during the session of the Rastriya Panchayat and during the period between the issuance of the notice of the summoning of the session and prior to the commencement of the session. But in accordance with the law providing for preventive detention, or in respect of any criminal prosecution they can be arrested.

In such cases the chairman of the Rastriya Panchayat shall be immediately informed by the officer making such arrest.

According to the constitution the breach of such privileges of the Rastriya Panchayat shall constitute contempt of the Rastriya Panchayat. And the Rastriya Panchayat shall have power to decide whether or not there has been any breach of such privileges. 'If a person commits contempt of the Rastriya Panchayat. the presiding officer of the Rastriya Panchayat may, by a decision of the Rastriya Panchayat, pass an order sentencing such person to a term of imprisonment which may, at the most, extent to the end of the session. But person charged with such offence shall not be punished without giving him an opportunity to show cause as to why he should not be punished. In such cases the officer presiding over a meeting of the Rastriya Panchayat has power to issue a warrant of arrest or a summons, to summon witness, to take evidence, to cause documents to be produced and to record statements. The remuneration of the chairman, the vice-chairman and other members of the Rastriya Panchayat shall be fixed by an Act and until so determined shall be as subject to the rules made by His Majesty. The Secretary of the Rastriya Panchayat shall be appointed by His Majesty.

Any member of the Rastriya Panchayat may introduce a bill in the Rastriya Panchayat though subject to the constitution and the rules of the Rastriya Panchayat. According to the constitution "before introducing any bill or amendment in respect of any of the following matters by a member other than a Minister of the Crown or a Minister of states or an assistant Minister prior Sanction of His Majesty shall be necessary and such sanction may be obtained through a Minister of the Crown or a Minister of state or an Assistant Minister:

1. Imposition or collection of or increment in taxation;
2. Appropriation or expenditure of amount or increment in the amount sought to be appropriated to expended out of the consolidated Fund or any other government fund;
3. Any matter relating to the Civil List of the Royal Family;

4. Any matter relating to the debt or guarantee for which His Majesty's Government is liable; or
5. Any matter relating to Royal Armed Forces.

No bill, which expresses in its preamble to have been made for the sake of public good to regulate or control the exercise of fundamental rights, shall be introduced without the sanction of His Majesty, And before giving such sanction His Majesty may consult the Raj Sabha.

Any bill passed by the House is presented to His Majesty for His assent. But the right, to give assent or not to give assent or to send back a bill with amendment to the Rastriya Panchayat is reserved on His Majesty. If His Majesty is willing to give His assent, He shall notify His assent ordinarily within one month of the presentation of the bill. If His Majesty desires to withhold His assent or desires to give assent with amendment to a bill passed by the Rastriya Panchayat He may, after consulting the Raj Sabha, return the bill to the Rastriya Panchayat with a message and the Rastriya Panchayat shall after giving consideration over such message, submit its recommendation to His Majesty as soon as possible and His Majesty after having considered such recommendations, shall finally decide whether to give or to withhold His assent or to give his assent with amendments. When assent is given by His Majesty to a bill such bill shall become an Act.

"Not only in monarchical form of government but even in Republican form of government this kind of right has been given to the Head of a state. In general it is practice every where including the United Kingdom. In Netherland Money bills are introduced only by the Monarch. In this respect our constitution is very liberal". His Majesty can issue an ordinance when the Rastriya Panchayat is not in session such ordinances are required to come in immediate operation or according to the circumstances. But they shall not be inconsistent with the provisions of the constitution. These Ordinances have the same force and effect as an Act.

Such ordinances shall be put before the Rastriya Panchayat

within 7 days of its sitting subsequent to such promulgation. His Majesty may withdraw such ordinances at any time. And these ordinances cease to have effect ofter the lapse of forty five days of the sitting of the Rastriya Panchayat if it is not withdrawn by His Majesty.

According to the constitution no tax can be imposed except under the provision of the constitution and Government will not take any loan except under such provision. The constitution has also made a provision for a consolidated fund. It is a public fund. Except His Majesty's private revenues, and trust funds and local taxes, all revenues received by His Majesty's Government, all loans raised on the security of the public revenues, and all moneys received in repayment of any loan made under the authority of an Act shall, unless otherwise provided by an Act, be credited to this fund.

According to the constitution the following expenditure shall be charged on the consolidated Fund:

1. Civil List of the Royal Family as provided by an Act;
2. The remuneration payable to the Chairman and the Vice-Chairman of the Rastriya Panchayat, the Chief Justice and other Judges of the Supreme Court, the Chairman and members of the Public Service Commission, the Auditor General, the Chairman and the members of the standing committee of the Raj Sabha, the Chief Election Commissioner and other Election Commissioners;
3. The administrative expenses of the Raj Sabha, Rastriya Panchayat, the Supreme Court, the Public Service Commission and the department of the Auditor General and Election Commission;
4. All charges relating to the debts for which "His Majesty's government is liable";
5. Any sum required to satisfy any judgment or decree made by any court against His Majesty's Government; and

6. Any other sum declared by an Act to be so charged.

In every financial year His Majesty shall cause to be laid before the Rastriya Panchayat an annual budget consisting of the estimate of revenue, the some required to meet the charges on the consolidated Fund; and the some required to meet the expenditure to be provided by an Appropriation Act. The sums required to meet the expenditure to be provided by an Appropriation Act shall be specified under heads and shall be included in an Appropriation Bill. If it becomes necessary His Majesty shall cause to be laid the supplementary budget before the Rastriya Panchayat. This Supplementary budget is introduced when the amount authorised to be spent for a particular service in the annual budget or if a need has arisen for expenditure upon a new services, or the expenditure made during that financial year is in excess of the amount authorised in the annual budget.

Any portion (upto one third) of the expenditure estimated for the financial year may be incurred in advance by an Act pending the enactment of the Appropriation Bill. This Vote On Account shall not be submitted until the Estimates of Revenue and Expenditure have been presented in the Rastriya Panchayat. And the expenditure incurred in accordance with the Vote On Account Act shall be included in the Appropriation Bill. There is also a provision of Votes of Credit (emergency fund) to meet any local or national emergency whether due to natural causes or the threat of external aggression or internal disturbance or otherwise. The expenditure incurred under the Vote of Credit Act shall be included in a Supplementary Appropriation Bill as soon as possible. According to the constitution a contingency Fund is provided into which shall receive from time to time such sums as may be determined by an Act. Unforeseen expenditure shall be met out of this Fund. The amount of the expenditure so met shall be replaced as soon as possible by a Supplementary Appropriation Act. Matters relating to the transfer of the sums appropriated for one head to another and financial procedures may be regulated by an Act.

In keeping with modern democratic tradition the Rastriya Panchayat also has a provision for Cemmittee stages. In order to pass a bill, it has to go through three readings and various committees; such as Steerring Committee, Select Committee, Estimate Committee and Public Account committee etc.

First Reading: The Chairman of the Rastriya Panchayat, before sending a proposal to reading, goes through its contents and decides whether it is a money bill or not. The Chairman sends the proposal with introduction. This is called first reading. And a date for second reading is fixed. Since it is a formal affair, there will be no discussion about the proposal at this first reading.

Second Reading: But after the first reading second reading takes place on the date previously fixed. Before the second reading takes place, if it is felt necessary the proposal is referred to the Select Committee. This Select Committee is an Adhoc Committee and is formed according to need. This Select Committe, if it feels necessary, can prosent proposal with amendments. In the second reading the proposed amendments of the Select Committee will be discussed at length. It is in this stage that the bill is thoroughy discussed on its aims and objects and principles, then it is sent to the steering committee for minute details. In the Indian Parliament also, after the first reading, the proposal is sent to a special committee and this committee, if it feels necessary, can send the bill with amendments.

In England this happens after the second reading.

Third Reading: In the third reading there will be general discussion about the proposal. In this stage the report of the Steering Committee is also read out. And at last vote is taken and the legislature approves or rejects the bill.

Money Bills are not sent to a committee. The whole house discusses over it. In every country they have adopted their own way over money bills.

In England or in India government introduces bills related

to finance. So other members of the parliament cannot table it. But in Nepal any member of the legislature can propose money bills. Prior to the introduction of such a bill they have to take assent of His Majesty through Minister or State Minister or Assistant Minister.

Ministerial Responsibility: According to Sir Ivor Jennings, "Ministerial responsibility to the House of Commons is thus the means of assuring that government is in tune with popular opinion." It is for this reason that the members of House ask different questions and ministers are bound to reply it. If representatives of the people are not satisfied by works and deeds of a certain minister they can bring a vote of no-confidence against such a minister. Thus Sir Ivor Jennings remarks that, "It is necessary that ministerial responsibility means only that a politician must be able to answer in the House of Commons for every act of administration." One of the features of the British parliament is ministerial responibility. And saying of Jennings can be taken as proof of this fact.

So the meaning of the ministerial responsibility is that ministers should act according to policy, rules and regulations passed by the highest representative body. So in the ultimate end any member of the House can put a question to a minister.

Any member of the Rastriya Panchayat can pose any question to a minister who is expected to reply. If majority members of the Rastriya Panchayat and two-third of present members pass a vote of no-confidence against the conduct of a minister, the minister has to resign. But His Majesty has to accept such a proposal. Both in England and in India no bill can be passed unless and until it has been given assent by the head of state. So it will be a political illusion if we argue that in Nepal ministers are responsible only to His Majesty.

In party system, party in power has to work according to its manifesto and meet the challange of its opponent, so ministelia responsibility is joint in this kind of government. This kind of responsibility in the words of Jennings is only a political responsibility.

From 1783 in England a principle was adopted according to which joint ministerial responsibility was recognised. And the spirit of the cabinet system was made subject to team work. To achieve this spirit it was accepted that ministers should belong to one political party. It is a well known fact that if a Ministry were to be composed of different political parties adhering to different political ideology this team spirit cannot be realised. It is an accepted fact that success of cabinet depends on its unity.

The American Congress cannot control the activites of the cabinet. No member of the American cabinet is a member of the congress so he cannot be responsible to them. Thus the US cabinet is responsible to the President alone. But in Nepal it will be a great mistake to say that Minister is not responsible to the House for reasons are that,

(*a*) Ministers are choosen out of the members of the Rastriya Panchayat, and

(*b*) every member of the House has right to question any Minister.

Those evils which made cabinet Ministers dictators in many countries are not present in Nepal for (1) the Ministers are responsible also to His Majesty and (2) there is no party system.

In party system, although in principle, members of parliament can pass a vote of no con-fidence against their leaders yet they do not do it for obvious reasons. But members of Rastriya Panchayat in Nepal are not tied by the rope of political parties so they are free to adopt a motion against any minister. This also proves that the Council of Ministers is responsible to the House.

In parliamentary system there is joint responsibility so if a vote of no-confidence is passed against a minister the whole cabinet has to resign. In the similar fashion cabinet can dismiss parliament. But Rastriya Panchayat is a permanent institution: it cannot be dissolved. So the question of joint ministeral responsibility to the House also does not arise.

In parliamentary system of government, in the term of the constitution, the head of a state appoints ministers. But in real practice these ministers are responsible to the legislature not to the head of the state. In the USSR, the Supreme Soviet appoints ministers. But in Russia ministers are not responsible to the Supreme Soviet and they cannot dissolve it. "If the Supreme Soviet rejects the policy of Council of Ministers no one has to resign. There is not a single instance to prove that a minister has resigned because the Supreme Soviet has disapproved a certain policy." The main reason behind this is that the Presidium is powerful enough in formulating policies. In this context, it will be interesting to compare and contrast the two systems.

The Panchayat system is not an immitation of either of these two ways. The Council of Ministers of Nepal is of its own kind although it has not rejected the merits of the parliamentary form of government. Ministers are members of the Rastriya Panchayat and any member of the House can move a proposal against any minister. In this sense, both the form of governments can be compared. But in order to check a minister from being a dictator they are made responsible to His Majesty also.

It is true that we have no cabinet system of government like in England. But it is also equally true that the USA has also no system like the Nepalese one. Both England and America have their own meaning of the term of ministerial responsibility, yet both are democratic in spirit. It is also the same thing to say that both the systems have their own way of ministers being responsible to legislatures. So is the case with Nepal. No body can deny the truth that modern democratic complexities are western in origin, but these problems are to be solved by one's own way.

For the success of any democratic system, the decentralization of administration and local-self governing bodies on which the decentralization is executed, are essential. In fact, no democratic system without local self-governing institutions can at all success. The success of local self-governing institutions is the guaze where with is measured the success of a democratic system.

Also in India, our neighbour country, where they have the parliamentary system, a special stress is laid on the decentralization of administration and the development of local self-governing bodies. This is done for the successful working of democracy. There the Panchayat is taken as a unit of the decentralization of administration, and special attention is paid to the development of Panchayats for the success of the parliamentary democracy.

To day in India, about 200,000 Gaun Panchayats are working on the principle of common good. The Indian 'Panchayat Raj' is put at three different levels, viz, the Gaun Panchayat (the village Panchayat), the Panchayat Samiti (the Panchayati Committee) and the Zila Parishad (the district assembly). In the Indian 'Panchayat Raj' system, the 'Gaun panchayat is the bottom unit. Above it stands the 'Panchayat Samiti. It is composed of members elected to it from the various areas of the development blocks. The 'Jilla Parishad' is the top level. The chairman of the jilla-panchayats, the M.P. from the area comprising the districts and the members of the State Legislative Assembly function as its members. This, we find that the Indian Panchayat system like the Nepalese counterpart, is put at different consecutive levels.

But in India the Panchayat institution exists as the units of local self-government, whereas in the Nepalese Panchayat system they function as the units of or the very foundation of the political administration. In India, the 'Panchayat Raj' and the parliamentary system keep separate identity but they co-exist. They have an aim at developing the 'panchayat raj' and making it altimately into a system of life of the Indian people. This aim has been mentioned in the Indian Constitution as a directive element. Mahatma Gandhi, the father of the Indian nation, also aimed at the 'panchayat raj' Mahatma Gandhi once said that "true democracy cannot be worked out by 20 men sitting at the centre: it has to be worked from bellow by the people of every village". All democratic ideals and principles have admitted it that real democracy should be consolidated from its very foundation.

The basic democracy, adopted in Pakistan after the failure of the parliamentary system, also follows the four-tire system founded on the Union Panchayat, directly elected at the village level. Thus, in Pakistan, they have:

1. the Union Panchayat,
2. the 'Tehsil' (Thana Council),
3. the District Council, and
4. the Division Council.

In this system, the lowest level is the union panchayat. Election for it is held on the principle of adult franchise. Generally, one representative from among 1,000 to 1,500 is elected. A union panchayat generally has 10 elected and 5 nominated members. Room has been created for the nomination of the 5 members, so this representation in the union panchayat has been extended there also to the woman and the farmers and those who do not put candidature but display special calibre for the service of the people.

Works relating to administration, justice, security of people's life and property and development, and, above all, national reconstruction works are entrusted to the union panchayat.

The level just above the union panchayat is the 'Tehsil' Council in West Pakistan, and the 'Thana Council' in East Pakistan. The chairman of each union panchayat automatically becomes a member of the 'Tehsil' or 'Thana Council'. If there is a municipality within the 'Tehsil' or 'Thana Council', the chairman of the municipality also becomes a member of the

'Tehsil' or 'Thana Council. This 'Tehsil' or 'Thana Council' concerns iiself principally with development works within its territory. It is for this reason that some 'Tehsil' and 'Thanas' officials concerned with development activities become, the members of those councils.

In the level order, next to the 'Tehsil' or 'Thana' stands the District Council where decisions on the issues concerning to the development of the district are made. The deputy commissioner is its chairman. "Since the development activities require the joint efforts of the 'government and the people, representation in the Councils will be on a fifty-fifty basis between government officials of the development departments and non-officials including members of the Union Panchayats".

The fourth and top level is the Division Council, of which the chairman is the commissioner. Again, non-officials concerned with nation-building departments are associated in equal numbers.

It is hoped in Pakistan, that the basic democracy based thus on four consecutive levels will create in the mass a general feeling of political awakening and the full sense of responsibility. There the awakening and the sense of responsibility constitute the basic requirement for the successful working of democracy.

The parliamentary system mainly exhibits two different organizational flaws. On the one hand, we find that in this system there is no direct relation whatsoever between the parliament, the supreme institution representating the entire population, and the institutions of local self-government, the very root of democracy, and, on the other, it does not perceive any broadness of representation.

In principle, majority rules over minority, but in practice minority rules over majority. Take for example the case of the Nepali Congress which won the general election of 2015 and thereby organised the government. In the election the Nepali

Congress obtained 37.2 per cent of the total number of votes cast, but in the parliament it secured about 67.8 per cent of the total number of seats. Thus, though the Nepali Congress got majority in the parliament, yet it could not obtain the majority in votes in the the general election. About 63 per cent of the votes were not cast in its favour. Notwithstanding it, the Nepali Congress itself obtained constitutional authority for organizing the government and thereby ruled over the majority. This particular organizational flaw can be ascribed to the very party system so much in vogue then.

Strees is laid on the expansion and development of the institution of local self-government so as to get quit of the first flaw pointed out above. So far as the removal of the other flaw is concerned, political scholars have not yet been in a position to effect it and have been satisfied themselves by taking recourse to extolling the parliamentary system. Ashirvatham, a celebrated political scholar satisfies himself, by saying, "What is the way out? Is there any other form of government which is as good as democracy, if not better? Our answer is negative."

But the Nepalese Panchayat system exhibits neither of the flaws. In Nepal local Panchayats are the sources of democratic spirit, and the democratic atmosphere owes its genesis to them. Representatives, with refined leadership and having acquired enough of the Panchayat experience, come forth as members of the National Panchayat, the supreme institution, from the bottom level, and through the two higher levels. Thus, because the local Panchayats are the sources and foundations of the National Panchayat, direct relation between them can strongly be affirmed. As the stem of a tree grows from the roots, its source and foundation; so does the National Panchayat grows from the local panchayats, its roots. It is the member of a local Panchayat who enters into the National Panchayat. Since the roots of democracy strike into the local institutions and grow in them the National Panchayat, which grows from them can be called the tree of democracy. It is for this reason that the organizational form of the panchayat system can be said to be fully cultured and democratic. In the parliamentary system, however, tradition grows the stem-the parliament, and then the roots-the Panchayats.

The Nepalese Panchayat system, which is partiless in character, there is no room whatsoever for disharmony of the majority obtained by the representatives with the votes cast in their favour, we have no intention to say that the Panchayat system itself is absolutely flawless; but any unprejudiced thinker may conclude upon by comparing the organizational forms, that the Panchayat system is definitely better than its parliamentary counterpart.

It is generally admitted that even in the parliamentary system self-government institutions, like the panchayats, are regarded as the foundations of democracy and the first schools for the development of rural leadership. Yet they do not have any harmonic or chain relation with the parliament, the supreme institution of representatives of the entire population; in other words, there exists no direct relation between the foundation and the mansion erected on it. But in the Panchayat system all the panchayats of the state stand in a chain relation to the National Panchayat, for which reason it can be said that the Panchayat system is founded on the principle of maximum decentralization of power—the decentralization based on national unity. Eversince the glorious day, Falgun 7, 2018, when the election for the village Panchayats commenced, they were subsequently followed by the elections for the district and zonal Panchayats, and the National Panchayat. Thus elections were held for as many as 3,646 village Panchayats, 14 city Panchayats (Nagar Panchayats), 75 district Panchayats and 14 zonal Panchayats, which finally led to the organization of the National Panchayat, the supreme institution.

In the opinion of a critic, there is an important flaw in the organizational form of the National Panchayat. He observes, "there is no provision for the whip as in the party system. The whip controls and guides the members of his party in the parliament. But because there is no provision for such a leadership in the National Panchayat, differences of opinions may arise among its members and in this context it may be difficult to come to a compromise, which may result in fractionism. The Chairman of the National Panchayat cannot be called its leader. He is but a presiding officer to conduct the meetings".

Such a comment touches only on the party system in a country where the party having won majority in the parliament, organizes the government. Where there is a continuous apprehension of the harm, that may rise out of fractionism within a party, and a constant fear of the resolution of non-confidence motion by the opposition parties, there the constitution has a provision for the leadership of the party majority in the parliament by an influential member. The main objective behind this provision is to tie up commonly all the members of the winning party, with a string of party unity. In the Nepalese parliament instituted in 2016, Mr. Vishwavandhu Thapa was the chief whip of the Nepali Congress, the winning party. But it has been noticed that even the whip has not been able to effect oneness of opinion among all the members of the parliament and that the impact of the whip, if we can say there has been any, could be detected only within the short compass of the party to which the whip belonged. We may, for example, trace back to what once happened when Nepal had the parliamentary system with a constitutional provision for the whip. The Nepali Congress then in power, had, by virtue of the majority it had obtained, passed even such bills in protest of which all the members of the opposition parties had in a body quitted the parliamentary meeting. The whip is deemed necessary on a definite principle and to meet a particular necessity. But the partiless Panchayat system attaches importance neither to the principle nor the necessity of a whip. The want of the whip in the National Panchayat, cannot, therefore be looked upon as a flaw.

The National Panchayat is a uni-cameral legislature. All political scholars do not emphasize the esssentially of the bi-cameral legislative system. And even in practice there is no uniformity in owning a definite number of houses. If countries like Britain, America and India have the bi-cameral legislature, countries like Turky, Finland and Portugal have the unicameral system. Whether the legislative should be unicameral or bi-cameral is still a matter of controversy. As a matter of fact for federal states and to a certain extent, for countries with party-systems, the bi-cameral legislature may be deemed necessary; but for a country professing partiless democracy, it is nothing essential." "Although the system of government in the Kingdom of Nepal is one that is unitary, yet the unicameral legislature—the National Panchayat—is so designed as so to include and harmonize the elements and the necessary merits of both the houses (bi-cameral legislature). This could be achieved on the principle of the decentralization of powers."

3

Democracy in Nepal

The history of present day democracy beings with the Parliament and the cabinet system of Great Britain. Among the present constitutions of the world, the British Constitution is the oldest. Similarly the Parliament of England is also called the mother of the parliamentary system. The influence of the Parliamentary system has been diffused throughout the world, from Canada and Australia to Sweden and South Africa. So while dealing with modern democratic administration one has not to forget to mention Great Britain.

The constitution of England has been gradually developing for the last 13 or 14 hundred years. In England no revolution did take place which can be compared with the French Revolution of 1789 and the Russian Revolution of 1917. The main reason behind the gradual development of [the constitution of England was that geographically she was differently located than the European continent and the people were more inclined towards reformations than revolution. It has been the speciality of England.

It was due to prolonged civil war that gave the idea of tolerance and peaceful compromise among the British people. Moreover the economic achievements, the victory in the two world wars and the construction of the great empire gave rise to the feeling of unity among the British people. All these are the result of a long period of development.

Many nations of the world take enough incentive from the British model, which in itself has been a product of growth. This tend of imitation from the British pattern went in increasing even up to the middle of this century. But that type of democracy could not flourish as much in those nations as it did in England. Since the political development of different nations do not move on a uniform pattern, there is no reason to believe that the British model of democracy can work with the same spirit everywhere. It goes without saying that the parliamentary system of Great Britain has its own effect in this world. But influence is one thing and pure imitation is another. For the success of a given system in a country many factors such as economic conditions, general awareness of the people, geographical conditions and historical background play a very influential role. All these factors determine the success or failure of a given system. Thus from political view point it will be gross mistake if we say that a particular system can work effectively in all parts of the world.

The parliamentary system of England can achieve success elsewhere only if in British like environment prevails there. So there is no reason of surprise if a typical British system does not work well every where. Even the Parliamentary System of Government which was originated in England cannot function well elsewhere, if some sort of local colour is not given to it. The constitution of India which was drafted after her independence, and which was amply influenced by the ideology of freedom from England and the United States of America has made the provision of the "President" in the US fashion rather than the provision of "Kingship" like the United Kingdom. But the Chairman of the Indian Constitutional Assembly Dr. Ambedkar had remarked, "The word "President" connotes with the President of the United States but except in word itself there is no similarity between the way of administrations of the US and of India." So, since there is no "Kingship" the system of India is not like a British one. Although the Indian

System of Government is different from the British and the American pattern yet no politician can call it undemocratic. Although India got enough incentive to establish a democratic form of government from Great Britain and the United States of America yet she could not copy exactly either of those two forms of governments. It is bccause of her own problems and conditions the Indian system is more like Indian rather than British or American.

In the 17th century in England like in any other parts of Europe religious strife took place. In order to get rid of this commotion and lead a life of peace many men from England went to settle in the USA. In the same way the British system gave a fresh impetus to the Americans. So after 1789 when the Americans got independence they established a democratic system of government of their own. England had adopted a monarchical, unitary and parliamentary form of government. But due to different environment the USA chose for a federal and Presidential form of government. But nobody can claim that the only democratic government is the British one and the American system of government is an undemocratic. A well-known learned man of political science, Mr Asirvatham has remarked thus, "Democracy and Parliamentary Government are not necessarily identical." So in a word the Parliamentary system is not the only democratic system.

The framers of the Indian constitution, taking lesson from the past history of India, wanted to make centre more powerful. And inspite of the fact that India has federalism, it is more like the Indian rather than the American one. The US constitution has empowered residuary powers to units. But the Indian constitution has given this power to the centre, so the centre is powerful. The Americans choose their own governors. In India the President nominates them. So the Indian federalism is different from the American or the Swiss federalism. Inspite of these differences nobody can say that in Great Britain, or in the USA or in Switzerland or in India there is nothing like democracy. Inspite of all these apparent differences the features of federalism like:

(*a*) supremacy of the constitution,

(*b*) divison of powers, and

(*c*) establishment of supreme court are common for the Swiss, the American and the Indian constitutions.

So there is nothing like universal truth in theories of political science. And any form of government worth of name should be run in accordance with the genius, tradition and geographical conditions of that nation. Before criticising a system of government it is necessary to go into details. Thus although the US system of government has no cabinet system or the British model has no President it will be mistake if we say that either of them are undemocratic. In this way we have to find out elements of democracy first. Only if a society is deprived of these features one has to condermn it as an undemocratic.

Inspite of some differences in the forms some special features are deemed necessary for modern democracy and in the absence of them democracy cannot function well.

Democracy is not a mechanical form of government. It is rather a medium which helps to develop the feeling of self-government. Democracy can flourish only when there is a favourable condition. In the absence of this democracy cannot work efficiently. In this connection it is important to recall the saying of His Majesty King Mahendra, "Democracy is not possible under rules and regulations only, the representatives of the people should develop a democratic attitude and similarly public servants also should execute rules efficiently."

The most important elements of democracy are freedom of speech and the freedom of press. Although the definition of Abraham Lincon "Government of the people, for the people and by the people" is popular yet modern political scientists define democracy as, "Government by discussion and compromise." Thus modern tendency is more towards expression of different views and after that they try to come out for an agreed compromise. But if somebody cannot get a chance of expressing his view there does not arise a question for a compromise. All most all the constitutions of the world have given very much importance to the right of freedom, much on the definition of democracy yet they agree unconditionally on the great role of freedom of speech. Even the Soviet constitution, Articles 125 sub-article (a) and (b) has made the provisions for freedom of speech and publicatons. In Western nations these rights are supposed to be the pillars of democracy.

But while utilising these important rights every individual should take into consideration his duty also. Rights and duties go together. Although all these rights are guaranteed by the constitution yet they are not unlimited specially when the question of social order takes place. It is also a way of democracy. Those persons who donot observe democratic principles they are not entitled for constitutional protection. As a matter of fact unlimited rights are not rights at all, it is anarchy. There is no constitution in the world which has not made any provision of control. In this connection it is important to recall that the American Supreme court has recognised many limitations.

Apart from these, there are certain other elements of democracy, on the basis of whose and whose alone true democracy can be established. These other vital elements are Constitution, Election on the basis of that constitution, provision of Public Service Commission and establishment of Supreme Court of the land. Once these basic elements are present democracy can very well flourish.

Viewed from this angle in Nepal all these basic prerequisites are already established and the country is heading rapidly towards true democracy. According to Jennings, in brief there are three meanings of democracy:

(*a*) People must be free

(*b*) People should have a right to elect their own representatives and

(*c*) rulers should rule according to wishes of people. If we observe very keenly in Nepal, we find that all these three elements are present and the country is thriving forward.

Parliament is meant for discussion, that is on the floor of the house the representatives of people discuss policies of government. This house is called differently in different places. In India it is called 'Lok Sabha', in the USA House of Representatives, in Switzerland it is called National Council, in England it is House of Commons and in Japan it is called the Diet. The constitution of Nepal of 2015 called it Parliament and the Constitution of Nepal of 2019 as Rastriya (National) Panchayat. The meaning of the word 'Panchayat' is to settle disputes by five elderly men. Its broader form is Parliament or Rastriya Panchayat. So the prime requisite of democracy is the provision of a supreme institution of peoples' representatives instead of any particular brand or name.

It was August 15, 1947 that India got her independence and she adopted a parliamentary form of government. Similarly in October 1, 1949 China establised a Republican form of government based on Marxian principles. Situated in between these two countries Nepal has been influenced by both of them. But it was due to the great mountains on the north that influence of the south became more visible. A wave of democracy swept throughout the length and the breadth of Nepal. The 104-year old Ranarchy was broken into pieces by the popular movement. This popular movement was led by the Crown. After the political movement of 2007, Nepal like India tried for a parliamentary form of government and it was after the general election of 2015 that parliament was established in Nepal. It is true that the Revolution of 2007 of Nepal was influenced by India and the Parliament was also established in a similar fashion. But the experience of Nepal has shown that only a system of government which is suited to the living and powerful institutions of this place and which takes into account the historical backgrounds can be beneficial to the nation.

Since the Western type of democracy could not flourish in Nepal, the nation was bound to accept the Panchayat system based on the soil and tradition of Nepal. Around 1951 it was the fashion of the world to accept parliamentary system for democracy. But the parliamentary system was in experimental stage in many hations of Asia and Africa. Our experience tells us that the parliamentary form of government is not the final system for the world. Seeing a tendency among developing nations for taking parliamentary system as the final form of government, Dr. Jennings had warned, "The British type of parliamentary Government cannot be flourished easily in different environment. It is because of difference in soil. Even a nation inhabited by the British like people, the parliamentary government can take a different shape". So those politician who ignore this vital fact are sure to repent in future. It is a historical fact.

Nepal has already secured a very good position among countries of Asia and Africa who have already discarded the Westminster type of democracy and adopted the one which is in conformity with the taste, tradition and temperament of the concerned people.

After 1951 the Nepalese people being tolerant made experiment with the parliamentary form of government for about 10 years. But the people came to the conclusion that the Western style of democracy is not the answer of the problems confronting the nation. His Majesty King Mahendra did very well understand the popular sentiment and took the historical step of December, 1960. In a ten year period of time (1950-51-1960 various steps, like the formation of coilation government, one party government, appointment of advisors and election were taken in order to settle down the unsettled political conditions of Nepal. But this sort of party-democracy could not deliver goods to the people. The ten years period in Nepal was a period of political instability. Almost all political parties declared that their aims were the establishment of democratic socialism or popularism or nationalism in the nation. A wave of public meetings and speeches swept over the country. But the people, on the other side said, "If democracy means talks rather than deeds, if democracy means empty promises to people, we are not in favour of this sort of democracy." It is because the people were indifferent to the party-politics that the historical incident of 1960 took place.

The Nepalese people had trodden a new way after the revolution of 1950-51. After the historical step of 1960 and under the able leadership of His Majesty the King the Nepalese people have prepared a broadway. And the way was inagurated on Baisakh 1, 2022.

Thus the way or the system adopted by the Nepalese people is very thick and thin to the custom and tradition of Nepal. So the Nepalese have chalked out their own way of life. Nepal has adopted a new way of life and many emergent nations of Asia and Africa can take something out of it. Sooner or later many countries have to think seriously over the Panchayat system.

Nepal, although small yet very pertinent in the map of Asia was hidden from the outside world during the Rana period. It was due to the international polities and the revolution of 1950-51 that she is known to many nations of the world today. Nepal, sandwitched between the two giant nations of Asia has been able to follow up her own independent course. In the present day history of Asia when many nations are facing difficulty the experience of Nepal is sure to throw much light on them.

The classical theory of democracy says that, "there is diversity in the interest of individuals. Thus to resolve differences the wish of majority must be granted. But this does not mean, "maximum benefit of greater number only". Every learned man agrees that the body is more important than its parts. But majority can derive more benefit by listing cooperation from minority rather than by supressing them. Dr. Jennings says that the theory of one man one vote has been accepted on ground that the idea of one person cannot be better than the other in the matter of public policy Democracy cannot flourish in a society where peole think in terms of personal superiority. History has proved that it was due to the heavy prevalence of the thinking that the party form of democracy could not function in Nepal. The partyless Panchayat, system which is above all these petty triffles indicates for a better and prosperous future of Nepal.

In the absence of political parties, under the Panchayat system of government the task of enlightening and educating the people lies on the shoulder of various class organisations and the members of the Panchayats. If members of Panchayats and various class organisations become inactive there will be a political vaccum in the country. Thus political vaccum is a great hindrance for the development of political consciousness of the people. Thus political vigilance is necessary to safeguard democracy and in the absence of it there can not be created healthy atmosphere for democracy. The democratic Nepalese people always sould be conscious of this fact.

There is a significant difference between parliament and the Parliamentary systems. In parliament members decide policies of Government. In a straight word Parliament means meeting place. Rastriya Panchayat is also a meeting place. But in Parliamentary system various political parties play the game of national politics. Majority party forms its government and it is collectively responsible to the parliament. Thus parliament should not be confused with parliamentary government. Since the Rastriya Panchayat is the supreme representative body of people, it formulates all public policies and it will not be exaggerated to call the parliament of the people. But partyless Panchayat system is not a parliamentary system.

Since members of village Panchayat reach the level of the Rastriya Panchayat through village assembly which directly elects its representatives, this system of government has advantage of direct democracy.

It has been claimed that advantage of the parliamentary system is that it represent various shades of public opinion. But many sections of people who do not like to reach the parliament through the medium of political parties always remain unrepresented. In order to fill up this deficiency many countries have made provision of upper house. But the Panchayat system has covered the gap by having representatives of different class organisations and a few nominees of His Majesty. In this way the Rastriya Panchayat has served the purpose of the both the upper house as well as the lower house very efficiently.

We cannot still claim that bi-camere legislature is good for all. Countries of this world have adopted unicamerialism or bi-camerialism according to their tastes.

Even in those countries where there are two houses people have questioned the utility and need of the upper house. Even in England people are asking the desirability of maintaining the House of Lords. Hardly one-third lords take part in discussions. In America Senate has more prestige than the House of the Representatives. The Senate is supposed to be the most powerful body in the world. In Britain parliament means both the Houses of the parliament. In England where parliamentary system of government prevails the position of the Crown is beyond any dispute. Thus pure imitation of political organisation of other countries is not possible; regional influence is unavoidable. It is for this reason that we have not to ask whether an organisation resembles its contemporary organisation in other part of the globe. We have to judge by the fact that whether it does suit a particular condition.

It is under federalism that we feel the need of upper house of legislature. In party system the second house is advocated on the ground that all bills will be scrutinized by experienced people. In federalism, the upper house represents various states. But in Nepal neither of the above mentioned factor exists and the Panchayat system has ruled out the need of a second chamber.

The Rastriya Panchayat being a continuous body and most of its members being responsible to zonal assemblies it has got all advantages of contemporary legislature of the world. Moreover, since it represents all parts of the nation equally, it has got all advantages of the house of representatives. In this sense it is called an ideal system. Different legislatures of this world have different names but in operation they are identical.

PARLIAMENTARY AND PANCHAYAT SYSTEM

History of today has borrowed much from the past events and it will be illogical to argue that the incidents of today will have no bearing in the history of tomorrow. This is the basic fact of progressive ideals. The principle of 'thesis', 'Antithesis' and 'Synthesis' of Dilectical Materialism is based on these facts. The history of yesterday turns into 'thesis'. The history of today, the result of yesterday's experience, results into antithesis and the history of tomorrow, the issue as the conclusion of the experience of the history of today and yesterday, takes the form of synthesis. This is very important for both the students of history and the political science. As a result and reaction of the 104 years old Ranaregime the party democracy came into existence in Nepal. Only as a result of the experience of this party democracy Panchayat system came into existence as the cultured democratic system. So the partyless democracy has been established from the analysis of the experience and achievements of the party democracy. This analysis clearly reveals us the fact that the Panchayat system has come into existence as the progressive and indispensible historical necessity.

Under the Parliamentary system of democracy which is based on party system politics is handled by parties and different parties want to drag people in their own line. In this state of affairs political parties make most ambiguous promises to enlist popular support in their competition with other parties. Politics of many nations today is handled by party and in all those nations political parties, in order to hold government and to get maximum support of the people, make various promises by using many dazzling devices. By these devices public opinion though indirectly, is influenced and such kind of public opinion, in real democratic sense, cannot be called a healthy public opinion. But in the partyless Panchayat system there are no such agencies to drag the people in their party interest. Therefore the people can select their representatives and think over the matter relating to national importance cool headedly. Thus one can say without any hesitation that Panchayat system is the refined form of democratic system and its success will surely tempt other statesmen of the world to follow up this pattern for the development of real democracy—which does not consist the defects of the Parliamentary system. The historical necessity of Asia and Africa after the world war was to have a system like this which could delegate powers and assign more responsibilities to the people. Parliamentary democracy based on party system is seen heading towards failure in different countries of Asia and Africa like Iraq, Egypt Pakistan, Syria and Lebanon. So these countries were forced to think over the possibility of having a new and refined form of democracy.

Partyless democracy is not completely a new thing for the world. In ancient time, Rome and Greek city states were also democratic but they had no political parties like of today. There was Republic in India during the Buddhist period and even in that period there were no political parties. But many learned men are of opinion that there was a good form of epmocracy. Those democratic states were not as bigger as of today. So in modern state, for the first time the partyless democracy has been experimented in Nepal. As a matter of fact, even the democratic system of the USA at first was party less. The framers of American constitution had thought the party system as unnecessary and had no confidence in party government. They had planned for a government which is free from party intrigues. It is for this reason that the American constitution does not accept the existence of any political party. Mr. Madison, one of the fathers of the American constitution has called party groupings as the violence of faction. It is for this reason that in the United States President is elected by the people themselves directly. But with the growth and development of political parties the election of presidentship, in practise has become an indirect one. So one can firmly remark that political parties are not the integral part of democracy and there is no element of truth in the saying that a system becomes undemocratic in the absence political party. Since there is no political party its defects also do not appear in the Panchayat system, therefore a healthy public opinion can easily be developed under this system.

The world renowned definition of democracy, i.e. "Democracy is the government of the people for the people and by the people", of Abraham Lincoln has become obsolete today for many nations adopting the system of indirect democracy. So the political thinkers of today are towards a new definition of democracy. As to matter of practice the definition of Lincoln is more applicable to Panchayat system rather than to Parliamentary system. The four-tired Panchayat system is like a big mansion of which the foundation begins with the village. Panchayats, so all can take part in the administration which actually is the aim of the Panchayat system. For this in the Panchayat system the principle of decentralisation of powers has been adopted.

In a democracy even in dealing with national problems a ruling party always gives far more importance to the interest of his party. Thus directly or indirectly party interest is always placed above the national interest. But the partyless Panchayat system, based on national unity gives first importance to nation's sovereignty. So a time has come to give up the tradition of handling the national politics through the media of political parties.

In a parliamentary system the politics of a nation is based on the party line and the party politics affects even the national interest. Different political parties have their own line. Even in a two party system of England, Conservative Party stresses more on competition among various industries while the Labour Party advocates for a control of industries to safeguard the interests of labourers and consumers. The option for a particular political party may affect the foreign policy of the country. While, if we give chance for only one political party to remain in power, there is always fear of turning it into a dictator. Moreover, there is a constant struggle between the party in power and opposition parties. The party in power tries to prove its opponent as the opponent of the people. Its obvious result is that many incidents take place and civil strifes flare up.

In a Parliamentary system representatives are chosen

on party basis than on individual capacity. So voting for A party against B means supporting the policy of A rather than that of B. But no political party represents all the members of the society. Even the vanquished party represents a large number of voters. In this wider context party democracy can be called a "rule of the victor-party or its supporters over the vanquished parties and their supporters". Party democracy can be called correctly, in the political sense that it is a government run by one group over other.

Majority scored by victor-party seems to be rediculous in the sense of real majority. A political party forms government of its own by virtue of the fact that it has gained one vote more than its opponent. Thus the margin of one vote makes a party 'victor' and other 'defeated'. In the real sense it is the misuse of 'majority'. According to Sir Ivor Jennings in the election of 1945 there were in all 33,065,000 voters in England. Out of them Labour Party scored 11,986,000 and formed a government of its own. So the Labour Party came into power gaining only 36.2 per cent of the total votes. Thus Sir Jennings concludes that this form of proportional representation establishes a government of a group of people instead of that of whole population. All these obviously are the defects of party system but in the partyless Panchayat system which is based on national politics these defects are characterised by total absence. And any sane man can give his opinion that a government run by majority of the whole of the people is more democratic than the one run by a group of population. In Parliamentary system there is no proper co-ordination between the position of different political parties inside the house and the real majority of the country. As for example is 1945 the Labour Party in England although scored only 26.2 per cent of total votes yet it could win majority of seats of the House of Commons and formed the government. Similarly in the general election of Nepal in 2015 the Nepali Congress could over 67.8 per cent of seats in the House although it had scored only 37.2 per cent of the total votes cast. The result of 2015 election and position of different political parties are following:

Names of the party	elected candidates	total votes scored
1. Nepali Congress	74	66,68,898
2. Gorkha Parishad	19	3,05,118
3. Samyukta Prajatantra Party	5	1,77,408
4. Nepal Communist Party	4	1,29,142
5. Nepal Praja Parishad (Acharya Wing)	2	53,038
6. Nepali Praja Parishad (Mishra Wing)	1	59,820
7. Tarai Congress	0	36,107
8. Nepali Rastriya Congress	0	12,707
9. Prajatantrik Mahasabha	0	59,896

Thus in parliamentary system a political party may score majority seats in the House of Representatives and thereby form a government of its own without getting majority of votes from the actual voters. This sort of queer majority can very well be defined as a mechanical majority. In such a case it is better to call the party-government that, "it runs a government because it has a majority of seats in the House and not because it commands majority of votes of the people". So many political thinkers opine that this practical weakness of party politics can be minimised only by curtailing the scope of political parties. The tendency of party politics is harmful and the success of democracy depends on the curtailment of unnecessary activities of political parties. And it is gratifying to note that the partyless Panchayat system has freed itself these difficulties. In the Parliamentary system in which the government is formed on the basis of the party majority it is the result of the devotion and belief in the party leader; so it is called his majority. In the coventional parliamentary system there is little room to discuss individual's character, honesty, service and calibre. Voters elect representative in the name of the party. So in the general election individuality of a candidate is less important than the policy of political party. In the name of the political party even a bogus candidate can win the election.

As a matter of fact the high hopes of parliamentary system have not been realised so far. Contrary to this the weakness of parliamentary system are growing day by day. So Mr. Ashirvatham, the well known writer of political science holds the view that if all these visible defects of parliamentary system cannot be removed there is every reason to believe that parliamentary system will be replaced by other form of government. This is a grave problem for those who have adopted conventional democratic system of government.

According to the critic of parliamentary system of government it stresses more to amount than merits. It is not a question that how many wise men have supported a particular party. It is just a question as how many people stand for a political party. So majority which a political party can enlists is mechanical in nature. Thus by a margin of a few votes one party rules over other. And Mill has rightly called it a tyrany of majority. No majority party can get all the votes of people. But this weakness does not lie in a partyless system. So in a partyless democracy voters can cast their votes without being pursuaded by big political party.

Democracy is an abstract word which has a very keen relationship with freedom, equality and fraternity. These three factors are also the contributions of the French Revolution of 1789. So for a successful working of democracy these three factors are important, but not the party system. Moreover, shape of democracy depends upon so many factors as tradition, experiences of the people, geographical conditions and socio-economic conditions of a country. And there is wide room to grow and develop these factors under partyless Panchayat democracy.

Party politics is based on limited self—interest of a particular individual or a party. So the party politics is always limited in comparisicn with the national interest. In a country where illiteracy is rampant political party turns out as a means of exploitation of people. Quarrels among various political parties obscure national political scene. Happily enough this question does not arise in a partyless democracy.

There was local autonomy in the former city states and a system of direct democracy prevailed there. But in the process of growth the size of states became larger and the system of representative democracy was adopted. The representatives, however, instead of being loyal to the people tried to mould the public opinion by foul means in a hid to reach in power by any possible means. Thus gradually party interest dominated the interest of common man. But in a partyless democracy interest of common man is predominant. In every village which comprises of a population of 2,500 to 3.000 there is one village Panchayat and 200 villagers can elect their own representative. So under the partyless Panchayat system the representatives can be in real contact with the people and be loyal to their electorates. Thus this partyless Panchayat system may be taken as a refined political philosophy of the twentieth century.

Under the party system those who can exploit the sentiment of people and take advantage of opportunity, rather than being loyal to people, succeed in public. But in the Panchayat system since constituency is small, the electorates can examine in details the merits and demerits of each candidates. So the candidates can not deceive the people by false promise. In the party system the representatives do not represent wishes of the people. They, in fact, represent the policy of their political party; and they take politics as a means of lively hood. So critics call this the "Evils of party politics". But in the partyless Panchayat system, based on national interest, these defects cannot arise.

In her long history of party democracy England transformed herself into a modern state without any great upheavals, in the class structure of society. But in Nepal with the begining of the parliamentary system of government great struggles arose in West No. I, Dang etc on the pretext of putting an end to exploitation. This also shows that every immitation cannot be fruitful.

The past history has shown that in Nepal, the party system did not encourage a sense of social service among people rather it facilitated narrow party feelings. This defect of the party system paved way for the partyless system of government in Nepal.

Although Bryee holds the opinion that political parties keep a nation's mind alive yet the experience of Nepal clearly shows the fact that the political parties have become a source of mental disturbances. So the saying of Bryce is not universally applicable, it only indicates the experience of a particular nation.

There was the time when an opposition party was supposed to be necessary in a parliamentary system. But this opposition party has turned out to be a faction. And Prof. Laski holds the view that the conflicts of political parties have endangered national unity. So the partyless Panchayat system is the best order on the way of maintaining national sovereignty.

In any political system the political shape, institutions and political theory are designed to achieve certain objectives. These targets are for an all round development of the people and national unity. Although there are various constitutional theories and shapes yet they aim to democratic. In Nepal the Panchayat system has been accepted as a constitutional theory and the institutions of our government; as in case of parliamentary government, the aim is the realisation for the good of an all round development of the people. In this Panchayat system also like any fully developed democratic system the members of the legislature are elected by the people themselves and the Council of Ministers is also formed out of the peoples' representatives. Moreover, the Nepalese people have accepted that through this system alone the development of the nation is possible.

The Nepalese people had experienced that the strife among various political parties did seriously jeopardise internal security. So the people found a great amount of truth in the saying of Prof. Laski that representative government can work smoothly only when people feel that security of the people is well guarded with. In the absence of a sense of security the very foundation of democracy i.e. tolerance is shaked. When a man is full of fear he can not settle every thing peacefully. So the system of government which is far away from class conflict is best of all and, if every people co-operate, any country can reach to the height of development comparatively in a shorter period of time.

According to Bagehot, the famous political thinker, following factors are responsible for the successful working of a representative government:

1. The political leaders should be in a position to enlist a whole hearted support from the people.
2. Any important section of the society should not be outside power.
3. The system should be devised in such a way that it must be based on nationwide tolerence.
4. and, the powerful majority party in power should not suppress the minority which is not in power.

An analytical study and a comparative point of view of the above mentioned four elements clearly reveal us the fact that the Panchayat system is more democratic than one which the country had before. In the partyless Panchayat system there is a good provision for electing the members of every class organisation; so the system can be well regarded as more comprehensive than a parliamentary system.

According to Prof. H.J. Laski the measuring rod of the success of parliamentary government is unanimity of opinion of all the political parties over fundamental issues. But it is not necessary here to repeat that the political parties of Nepal had no unanimity of opinion.

In the absence of political parties there can be a direct election. And where there is a system of direct election democracy can be all the more pure. So political thinkers opine that wherever it is possilbe party politics should be minimised.

According to Mr. Ramsay Mair, the famous British political thinker, multiparty system does away with violent oscillation and strikes a golden balance. But a 250 year old history of polilical parties has given us the lession that there cannot be a golden balance and a logical compromise in the party system is almost impossible. Even if a compromise could be reached it was not lasting. All coalition governments have become only temporary way out. In this connection it is worth recalling the remarks of Prof. Laski that in France where multiparty system prevailed the parliament could not be as famous as *it* is in England. It is known to all of us that France is like a house of political parties and because of this multiparty system many governments failed in France. So no person can claim that this tendency of the political party is conducive to the healthy growth of democratic feeling. E. Ashirvatham has gone even to a far extent, he says, because of the multiparty system, governments in France had a short life. And one of the great reasons of France's defeat with the Nazi Germany was the prevailing multiparty system :

Affter the end of the Civil War in England in the 17th. century the position of political parties has been strengthened. This party system was widely imitated throughout the length and breadth of the world. And those countries who had adopted parliamentary system also did accept the system of political parties as the basis of the parliamentary system. From the 18th. century onward the opposition party, in England, has been accpted as a necessary part of the constitution. But an opposition party always tries its level best to derive great benefit from the mistakes of the government and always misleads public business. But in the absence of such narrow interested political parties in the Panchayat system people can deliberate on national problems without any outside and undesirable pressure.

The justification of the existence of political parties is that they safeguard interest of different classes. Stalin, the leader of Marxian communism holds the view that, "In the USSR there is only one political party because there are not various classes. And in a classless society there is no need of political parties to represent any class." But in a society where there are different classes and if the the interests of those classes can be safeguarded even without political parties the democracy can work properly. Even in England where different political parties are working—according to Jennings there is no separate political party of 'farmers for the simple reason that the interest of farmers and landowners is not mutually antagonistic. As a matter of fact, political party is such a channel which carries popular aspiration and wishes upto the government level. So if the class organisations or the Panchayats can safeguard the interest of people there is no need of separate political parties. In the party system, in actual practise political parties cannot represent the wishes of all classes. This is the fundamental weakness of the party system. But in the partyless Panchayat system there is a provision and all important sections of the society are properly represented. So one can say that under the Panchayat system different sections of the nations are adequately represented.

In parliamentary system representatives are elected on the basis of popular vote. But if the voters are not politically conscious they can be easily misled. Sir Ivor Jennings has rightly pointed out that the general roters are pursuaded emotions by parties rather than by facts and figures. In this sense political parties are called the means of propaganda. So in a country where people are not well literate and political consciousness is lacking political parties pave the way for the degraded form of democracy. In such a condition according to E. Ashirvatham party dictatorship can be established.

According to Jennings the idea under the Nazi Party in Germany was that the people are no beeter off than animals and they can be directed in any way that one likes. But educated and conscious people cannot diverted easily. No politically conscious man thinks that he can be off duty by casting his vote. But in the Panchayat system in the absence of political party, each representative his direct relation with the village Panchayats, the lowest level of the system, so these evils can be nitigated to a considerable extent.

According to Jennings an average voter in England sees all the political parties with an eye of suspicion. A voter has no full confidence on any candidate yet he votes because he has to elect either this or that candidate. Inspite of this in England there is a closer relationship between government and people because of the prevailing civil liberty there. Civil liberty is a fundamental master which is the result of political independence. This political independencc is an outcome of a long development. The result of civil war in England was that the idea of religious toleration sprang up. And this tolerence is the basic factor of the English democracy. This is the feature peculiar to the English people. But this peculiarity is not visible in those countries who have imitated the British pattern of government. In the partyless Panchayat democracy, which is based on class harmony the concept of toleration can be developed well.

The main ideas of civic liberty are that the state should not discriminate people on grounds of proverty, social status, race, religion and so on. The concept of civic liberty also does not allow that a few people should be sacrificed for the benefit of many. These are also the fundamental concepts of the Panchayat system of democracy.

One of the high ideals of civic liberty is the election of representatives. There can not be a free election in the absence of rights to speak and to assemble. The constitution of Nepal, (2019) has guaranted both these rights in the article 11, clause (2) sub-clause (a) and (b) Thus one can easily say that in the Panchayat system civil liberty has been given an important place. The main problem of democracy is the representation of of the interest of all classes of society which does not necessarily mean representation only through any political party or parties. So there is no logic in the saying that in a democratic society political party alone is capable of representing people. Political parties often divide people and intellectuals of a nation. In this perspective any partyless democratic system unites that the various groups of the people and the intellectuals and unity of a nations stands far more superior than a party democracy.

Party democracy is quite expensive. So in poor underdeveloped countries this system does not help to improve the condition of the people. So from economic point also the party system cannot be appreciated. It is often argued that party system maintains harmonious relation between the executive and legislature, for the simple reason that the political party which commands majority in the parliament forms its own ministry. But in the United States of America member of the executive need not be also a member of the Congress. So there is not a harmonius relation between the two as was in England, Inspite of this difference the USA is as democratic as England. Even though we accept the logic in favour of the party system. we cannot reach at a conclusion that in order to establish a harmonious relation between executive and legislature the presence of political party is necessary. Contrary to this, in order to establish a good relationship between the two wings of the government there should be a provision that a member of the executive should be also member of the legislature, or if the legislature wants, it must be in a position of expelling the member of the executive. The Panchayat system has established a nice order that only the member of legislature (Rastriya Panchayat) can be member of executive (the Council of Ministers) and if honourable members of the Rastriya Panchayat so wish they can pass vote of no-confidence against any member of the Council of Ministers. For this provision has been made in the Article 26, clause (3) sub—clause (d) of the Nepalese constitution of 2019 (1963). Thus the Panchayat system has established a harmonious relation between the executive and the legislature.

Staunch supporters of the party system argue that political parties play a vital role in making government strong in parliamentary system. And in non-parliamentary system also political parties play a big role in determining public opinion. But the experience of France has belied this. France is often called a home of political parties. But because of this predominance of various political parties no government could stand there for a long time. The long history of political parties has more than adequately proved that in a country where party psychology is less dominant government can be more stable.

Whatever may be the great benefit of party system the parties have common objective of being in power by any means. So political parties always try to enlist more supporters. It is for this reason that at times of election such "promises are made which are never meant to be fulfilled." Thus in a country where people are ill-educated and illfed, various political parties, iu order to meet their selfish ends, do not put real facts and true and uniwisted policy before the common mass. This tendency of the political parties in underdeveloped countries cannot encourage and influence the fundamental element of democracy—the General Will.

So a comparative study of the Panchayat and Parliamentary system reveals that they have many common aims and objectives and their institutions also do not differ much. But there is also fundamental and significant differences between the two, that is the "Party System." In the process of development of party system it was generally felt that party system and parliamentary are synonimous or inseparable. So it was of course natural that everybody looked at the partyless Panchayat system with an eye of curiosity. In many underdeveloped countries of today parliamentary system has simply failed. One of the reasons of this failure of the parliamentary system is due the defects of party system and the total absence of political is a fundamental feature of this Panchayat system. This difference is important which makes' inspite of so many similarities between the two, this Panchayat system fundamentaily different from the Parliamentary system. According to modern way of thinking a government by the representatives who have the popular support of the majority of the people, is called a democratic government. But the Panchayat system has been hailed not only by majority of population but by all the Nepalese. No former government of Nepal received so much of public confidence as the Panchayat system has got.

We can say without any hesitation that for the condition of today the Panchayat system is the best suited as a form of government for Nepal. It is a bitter fact that the Parliamentary system could not stride forward with the development of the country and was completely failure in meeting national problems. In comparision with developed countries of the world we are lagging far behind. But we cannot remain idle. So we have to adapt a system of government by which we can develop our country in a short span of time. To attain this high novel aim we have completely discarded the system of government which had divided the people and intellectuals of the nation. And we have developed a system of government which unites hitherto scattered and divided forces of the nation. Therefore the Panchayat system is the demand of time and condition of the nation.

Another equally important matter is that every system of government possesses some good elements as well as weakness. Any system of government can be said good comparatively. So when we say that the Panchayat as a system of government is good, it is in relative sense of the term not in absolute sense. In conclusion we only can say that keeping in view of tradition of Nepal and temperament and genious of Nepalese people the Panchayat system of government is likely to be far more beneficial than the parliamentary system. Parliamentary system alone is not the form of democracy, so the failure of the Westminster style of democacy does not mean the failure of democracy as such.

4

The Parliamentary System in Nepal

Imitation of Others

The present form of democracy had already developed itself in the very beginning of the 19th. century and by the middle of the 20th century that is after the end of the Second World War, it flourished in a spectacular way. A deep sense of freedom swept the whole Afro-Asian continents, with the result that a number of countries gained independence. Since encouragement for their political freedom was received from others, those dependent countries after attaining political freedom imitated the political order of others without considering their cultural heritage, social and economic factors. This was the case with the system of government adopted by Nepal in 1950-51. But after gaining political independece the Afro-Asian countries found themselves in a wretched condition. In most of these countries the stereotype of Western democracy failed to serve the economic and political interests of the people.

In Nepal also experiences of 10-years period proved that the party system of government was unsuited for the country. But this does not mean that either the parliamentary system of government or the party system is bad in itself. Even under the parliamentary form of government people in some parts of the globe are inhaling an air of independence. On the contrary in Asia and Africa the Westminster type of democracy has posed a great challenge to the nations. Thus the main task lying ahead of these people is to help strengthen freedom owned from colonial powers by devising a system which in fact tallies with their own conditions. How to devise that new system is the burning question of day for them. Since the happenings of the past decades show that the stereotype of Western democracy cannot work in these countries, they have either to follow a communist type of government or find out a third way. Here it is worth recalling the words of Ayub Khan the President of Pakistant that, "We, the Pakistani people have finally come to the conclusion that a formal acceptance of the Westerntype of democracy is not be all and end of all our aims and aspirations so we have developed democracy from below."

Hollow Economic Slogans

Inspite of economic backwardness, due to unfavourable geographical and political factors, since the Crown had played the role of leader in the popular movement, a sense of reform pervaded the whole Kingdom. For political development a corresponding economic growth is a must. All Asian and African nations woke from the deep slumber of colonialism, but to protect their political freedom they had to encounter many hardships and ultimately the Westminster type of representative government simply failed. Reason behind this failure is the underdeveloped economy of the country. In the pre-industrial revolution period in England, democracy in its process of growth had to face many difficulties. There with the dawn of the modern democracy, the historical Industrial Revolution gave a fresh impetus to the tempo of economic growth resulting that the standard of living of the people recorded a high growth. But the history of the underdeveloped nations has made it a crystal —clear that in the absence of a viable economic base a political system borrowed from others cannot well-work.

This historical fact stood again in the way of parilamentary system then installed in Nepal. It would have been quite good in the interest of the prevailing government, if they had stressed for a gradual development of economic means rather than mongering a slogan of economic revolution. But the parliamentary government, within a year of the general election raised the voice of economic revolution. Not only this, the class conflicts which took place in West no. 1, Dang and so on was supported under false name of economic revolution.

In 2017, Sravan 25, a member of Mahasabha (Upper House) in reference of sending a fact finding commission to West No 1 had said, "The struggle has taken place agaisnst the exploitation and Nepali Congress whole-heartedly supports it."

During the discussion another member had remarked that, "If government is not afraid of this proposal (for sending a five-member committee) it must be approved."

And another member had expressed his view that "If the struggle is in between the exploiters and exploitees the government must take a firm action."

All these three remarks enable us to form our own opinion about the approach of the government in the West No. 1 incident Those incidents which took place in West No. 1 and in other parts of the Kingdom were not wiihin the control of the elected government. So they adopted a sceptic policy; they supported labelling it as a natural struggle, waging between the haves and have-nots. The then government could not grasp that the problem of Nepal is a problem of production not of a distribution.

Experimental Stage

As a matter of fact parliamentary form of democracy has not fully developed in any part of the world. It's success is a relative matter. The parliamentary system is in an experimental stage in all the countries who have adhered to it. In England, the birth place of the parliamentary government, also this system is still in the process of growth. In spite of the experiences of many centuries, in England only in the 19th. century the idea of the modern democracy arose and it was only in 1948 that the idea of one man one vote could be realised, which these days is popular even in Nepal and India. The women are entitled to vote in the USA from 1920 and in Britain from 1928. After attaining political freedom, India, Pakistan, Burma and Ceylon had imitated the Westminster style of democracy, but within a brief period of one and half decade they took it differently. The parliamentary system could not grow in the above mentioned four countries in the same speed.

The Plant Could not Germinate

After 1950-51 Nepal has steadily advocated for democratic principle. But the system of democracy which was installed in the country was quite a new thing for the people. Moreover to adopt permanently an allien way of life, self control and far-sightedness are the pre-requisites. Democracy is a tender plant which can take its root firmly only when people are prepared to be patient and sympathetic towards it. The so called leaders of the party-government could not understand that unnecessary hastyness may uproot the very existence of the plant. The leaders' shortsighted and ill-thought actions created suspicion in the minds of the people.

Party Interest

England has a long history of political parties. And there the political parties are the product of environment i.e. they have come as a complement. In England, history of different political parties is as old as the British constitution. After the Industrial Revolution in England the Labour Party appeared on the scene to represent trade unions and the workers of different industries. So the Labour Party came into operation to fill up a vacnum. But in Nepal many political parties appeared having no mission to full-fill. Every political party instead of taking the task of helping the masses had engaged in the task of gaining power politics. A man in the street was compelled to think that political party is a miracle to make ministers. The history of Nepal covering a period of 1950-51 to 1960 shows that:

1. Basis of the various political parties was not the popular consent.
2. The political leaders seriously lacked experience.
3. The political parties did not represent the ideals of the people. So no political party was the mirror of the people's aims and degree of consciousness. In a nutshell they were not fit to provide the needs of the people.

Moreover, their actions have amply proved that they were more interested to full-fill their parties', or personal ends. Almost every political party had parties within party. I was matter of pride to be leftist-oriented. Its' evil impac was also fet on class organisations. Each group tried to downgrade the other. There was no morality in the strict sense of the term. So one can deduct from all these that the party system was surrounded by all the evils like, narrow self-interest and greed for power which are contrary to the spirit of true democracy.

Lack of Toleration and Compromise

The history of political parties of Nepal has made it clear beyond any doubt that the two ingredient factors for a successful working of democracy viz. the idea of tolerance and compromise were totally lacking among the political leaders of the day. A little difference of opinion was enough to start a new political party in the country to reach the height of ministership. This is a fact proved by the Nepalese history after the period of 1950-51.

An important member of the dissolved Congress Party and the ex-member of the Rastriya (national) Panchayat, Mr. vishwabandhu Thapa has nicely written that, "One political party broke into different parties and each of them had a corresponding parallel party within. Looking at the number of political parties and considering the number of their leaders, a fear lurked behind as to whether the very existence of the country can be maintained at all .... Political parties were just like the clubs of ex-ministers." Mr. Thapa goes on, "After attaining power it (the Nepali Congress) forgot its election manifesto. It broke promises made before the people."

In the United Kingdom due to various religious struggles at last a sense of toleration and compromise did arise but in Nepal in the absence of that in a shortest possible time a large number of political parties were born. Its obvious repereussion was that, in Nepal the available intellectuals and manpower resources were divided against themselves which endangered national unity and political stability in the country. Now, one can well expect that the present partyless Panchayat-system will unite all those divided forces and develop a democratic system based on national solidarity.

Failed to Solve day to day Problems

The party government proved quite incapable even in the task of restoring peace and security in the country. So keeping in view, the party system of government, a challange to national integrity, was thrown and an unholy attempt of dragging the Crown in the dirty game of politics attempted when His Majesty the King, "in order to do away with the century-old poverty, ignorance and backwardness of the people" undertook the historic step under his own leadership. Time has shown that the move is in consonance with the real aspirations and aims of the public. Every one welcomed the historic step by heart and soul.

Indifference Towards duty

A man who is not conscious of his own duty can do very little for his society. Almost one year before the historical step was taken, on Magh 16, 2016, His Majesty the King has warned to the so called elected government in his famous Nepalgunj speech, pinpointing the government's indifference towards the general well-being. But the government paid no heed to it. Disturbances and irregularities were the order of those days.

So His Majesty the King was compelled to undertake the historical step, to save the people from dangers.

His Majesty the King had well cautioned the elected government in time. He said, "We have to develop the country by taking adequate measures which can tally with the general condition and culture of the country. It was by the whole, hearted support extended by the people, which has made possible to lay the foundation of democracy and the holding of general election in the country, But all this does not mean that, in the name of democracy people and the country should unnecessarily bear hardships, industries in the country may decrease, justice be costly and time consuming, bribery be rampant, unemployment be increased and those who are in prower look after anything excepting their own self-interest. The Nepalese people together with their rights have also certain duties to fulfil. Realising this, let every Nepali move in a cooperative manner so that in order to ful-fil my duties I may not be forced to take other step Let it be clear to all that I have also certain obligations they are to guard sovereignty and nationalism of the country and protect developmental works. If any real danger arises on its way I am fully determined to take a decisive step at any moment and at any cost. I only expect support from every Nepali people." The timely speech clearly testifies the fact that the historical step of December 15, 1960 was not taken at random. The Royal takeover was the sequel of actions of the elected government.

A casual reader may feel the speech of December 15, 1960 accidental but closer analysis reveals that it was the sequence of speeches and messages made and delivered by His Majesty the King from time to time. He had already pinpointed the mistakes of the elected government. He had also delivered a speech informing the people that the elected government had no magic rod and people must be patient. That was meant to encourage the elected government. His Majesty the King had again advised the elected government to follow a democratic pattern and that no one should drag others into a pit, since there was always a fear of falling down oneself into it. After completing the official tours of Japan and the United States of

America, His Majesty had expressed his deep sorrow over the West No. I incident and ordered the elected government for a proper handling of the whole show. On the eve of departure to the United Kingdom he had reminded the responsibility of a government that is, maintaining law and order in the realm and had condemned narrow personal interest. At last on Kartik 25, 2017 on the eve of Revolution-day message the King had condemned those who were in power and barter with the blood of martyrs. In such a horrible condition His Majesty had no other alternative except to use the rights conferred on him by the constitution. Other Royal messages also have made it clear that since the elected government did not honour the advices and warnings of the King he was forced to take the decisive step.

In the historical speech of December 15 His Majesty had declared that since the government did not pay any attention to his 'gesture' implementation of a firm step was necessary even to protect democracy itself. Not only people and opposition parties but even those who were the members of the Nepali Congress and were also in power had condemned the government. In such a grave situation the only ray of hope was the Monarchy and the only alternative, to save the country from danger was to use the rights provided by the constitution. Since every step of the Koirala-government was like the harbinger of national crisis, His Majesty was left with no option.

Lack of Common Sense

The political leaders were more emotional rather than intellectuals. And according to one critic they were more revolutionary than democractic like the one who always thinks and writes of changes. Political irrationality had reached the height to such an extent that they welcomed their liberator, His Majesty Tribhuvan, with black-flags, while he was on his way to Switzerland for medical treatment. In this way the socalled leaders dealt with the person who emancipated them. A well known writer Sri Krishnamurti writes, "Their Majesty's perfidy climaxed when a handful of them skulkily waved black flags on the eve of his departure to Switzerland for treatment. The incident left scar on his heart."

Took its Natural Course

Like anything else political philosophy has also its own days. Parliamentary system in Nepal died, reasons for this according to Y.G. Krishnamurti are the inappropriate and inadequate leadership. He traces out following reasons for the failure:

1. In the first place there was no rudiments of political organisations.
2. There was not a group of elite to bring about political and social changes.
3. The political parties were a hotbed of dissent and intrigue.
4. All the political leaders were fully integrated to some outside ideological establishment.
5. Although the new group used to talk about utopian ideals yet in practice they followed the foot-prints of the Ranas.
6. Groupism and personal self interest were rampant.
7. As against the verdict of history they enjoyed in abusing God and King.
8. A leader instead of addressing the King by well established order, that is "Your Majesty" even did not hesitate to pronounce, "Hello, Mr King."
9. Personal ego was the next factor for the failure.
10. The Nepali Congress forgot even the definition of "democracy".

The conclusions of Sri Krishnamurti make it clear that there was no single leader capable to prepare ground for the proper working of democracy. So to train these leaders in disciplinary matters, social and national services and give lessons on democracy the need of a national leader was keenly felt in the country. If one has the courage of appreciating facts the conclusions drawn by Sri Krishnamurti must be accepted without hesitation.

Negligence of Party-Principle

The political history of the world has shown that since the people in underdeveloped countries are illiterate and their living condition is poor, the party system is not suited for them. So in a country like Nepal the failure of party system is least surprising. The main aim of a political party is to "represent the well-being of the people and work as a middleman between the people and the government. The main elements of the political parties are social service and confidence of the people. But in Nepal where political parties had no history, their main aim was the attainment of power.

Unsuitable for Underdeveloped Nations

The experiences of backward countries have shown that in the absence of literate masses and economic development, the Western style of democracy cannot function. In such countries, that system of government alone can properly work which the average people can easily understand. Time has come and this hard fact must be accepted by all without a hitch. If democracy meant for the prosperous and clean life of the people then there is no need in quarelling about the political terminology, any name which can easily deliver them the desired goods is worth accepting. Although the political organisations of Nepal, India and Pakistan differ in names, their goal is the same-realisation of an ideal state where all round development of the people can be realised. The sayings of His Majesty King Mahendra, "Our ultimate aim should be strengthening the basis of democracy by adopting any means" and, "I always adhere to that type of democracy which we can follow well, which saves our nation and large number of people can be happy and prosperous; this is only a true democracy.", It shows that the Westminster type of democracy is not the only style of democracy in the world. The wise sayings of His Majesty the King also encourages every country to accept that form of government which is in accordance with their needs.

Over Ambition

It goes without saying that most of the leaders of the then political parties were revolutionary in minds and had sacrificed every thing they possessed for the sake of democracy. But with the dawn of democratic era in the country their only strategy was to become a minister and after that a legendary leader of history. So a stage had come when they changed into selfish creatures and the need of a leader who could guide them well arose. Not only this, according to Sri Krishnamurti a leader's strategy, was, "Aimed at pushing off the King and emerging out of the political chaos as a dictator.' This over ambition of leaders directed country in wrong direction.

According to another writer the party-government could not realise the following hard facts:

1. Democracy cannot flourish without popular consciousness.
2. Democracy cannot function well without stressing the importance economic development of the country.
3. People should be trained from the lowest level for proper working of democracy.
4. For a small nation which is sandwiched by two big countries party democracy becomes a death-knell.

According to the writer the party government within a period of 18 months could not teach us anything except the above mentioned lessons.

Foul Play Between the King and his Subjects

According to Sri Yadu Nath Khaual, the political parties who had full-freedom in the country for a period of ten years, tried to create antagonism between the King and his beloved subjects. So far the realisation of social and economic principles is concerned the political parties were utterely failure.

Sri. Khanal goes on, "A thorough reading of our history, historical developments, and study of other monarchical countries have led us to the firm conclusion that Kingship on one hand political and economic reforms on the other need not necessarily be antagonistic." In the world of today if there are progressive monarchies there are also conservative republics. The only avenue left for the development of Nepal is the prevailing closer relation between the King and his people. This is the only means for our development. To play a foul game between the King and his subjects is simply a political irrationality.

Since every nation has conditions peculiar to it no one can prescribe universal political institution. Our way of development is our own, which has become possible by the active co-operation subsisting between the King and his citizens.

All these above mentioned facts have been verified by history and no sane man can neglect it. Even if some writers try to evade it is impossible since history has not repeated itself.

5

Ideology and Democracy

It is not easy to give a precise definition of any political philosophy. Nobody, without taking into considerations of political aspect and many other relevant factors, can give definition and scope of a system. But a closer study of the foregoing chapters may amply reveal true concept of the Panchayat philosophy. Every political system has its own basis which gives rise to its philosophy. So in order to know the details of a political philosophy one has to go deep into its background.

That the basis of Karl Marx's socialism was class struggle and the background of the parliamentary system was the prevailing divine right theory of the Middle Age and the Renaissance gave the concept of the representation of the people incredes to safeguard their interests, whereas the foundation of the partyless panchayat system lies in the experiences gained from the parliamentary system of the government established in the country and working of various types of mono-party bi-party and multi-party governments in the world as a whole. So there are two main bases of the Panchayat system—tradition and experience.

His Majesty King Mahendra gave a new political philosophy out of the age old order of the Panchayats. This Panchayat system is very well based upon the will of the people and since the time immemorial it has been constantly filtered by the experiences of the people. That the last report of any system is the popular will and any system based on this consent is a real democracy. Since the Panchayats are directly responsible to the people, Sir Charles Metcalf has expressed his opinion that in the Village Panchayat all the gocd things of democracy are available. All the evils of the parliamentary system which made it unsuccessful in many parts of the world are characterised by their total absence in the Panchayat System. Thus the Panchayat System contains only good aspects of parliamentary government.

That the very foundation of the Panchayat System is common people. There is no political party as such, and that the Panchayat is a part of the Napalese culture, indicate that the aim of the present system is to create a healthy society. The pillars of parliamentary system are :

1. Adult franchise,
2. peoples representation, and
3. the party system.

But as mentioned beforehand a political party is not a part of democracy—party system is the outcome of an accident on its process of development. In the Panchayat system there is no political party but the presence of local self-government has strengthened the philosophical angle of the system much.

Since all the requisites of democracy are developed from the village level by the local institutions. Even in the parliamentary system of government village panchayat is called the school of democracy. It means the village panchayats are taken as the basic units of the political organisation. In the parliamentary system, in the centre there is a parliament and at the bottom village panchayats are developed. On the contrary under the Panchayat system the village panchayats are elected and developed to prepare ground for the system. And on this very basis of the village panchayat three other tires of the

Panchayat are developed—at the top being the Rastriya (national) Panchayat; like the parliament in the Westminster style of democracy.

In this way the Panchayat system can be compared with a building of having a solid foundation whereas a parliamentary system is like a house whose foundation-stone is being laid afterward. It goes without saying that the system which stands on a solid basis is far better than the one which has not it. It nas been widely accepted that the true foundation of democracy is the localself-government and in the absence of it development of village democracy is not possible. This has also been widely cherished that democracy, in order to work smoothly, has to take its root from below. In order to achieve this in the conventional type of democracy a great importanct is attached to the local self-government. Even in England, where the parliamentary system has developed to a greater extent, it has adopted a sound system of local self government. India has also adopted a parliamentary form of government but she at the same time has set an ideal of establishing Panchayatraj in the country. So local self government is like the solid foundation of a house which help stand democracy. In the democratic set up of today the village panchayats have turned into a good instrument to implement the policy of decentralisation.

The Panchayat System based on the ideals of democracy has also come out in the form of a political philosophy. The local self-institutions are the basis of the parliamentary philosophy but not the basis of the system. In the parliamentary form of government local self-government is developed as a separate wing. But in the Panchayat system on the basis of the delegation of powers, the local self-government is taken as the basis of the order.

In the Panchayat system and under the policy of decentralisation of powers the election of the village panchayats are undertaken as a part of the system. So one has to accept without any reservation that the Panchayat System is more democratic than the Parliamentary one.

Centralisation of powers vitally affect people in the utilisation of their rights and inhibit political organisations for their proper growth. In this wider context the Panchayat System of democracy can be called a refined stage of democracy. Even in party system of democracy a great importance is given to the theory of decentralisation of powers. But, since the very inclination of the party system is towards imposition of authority from above and majority party rule over the country, the theory of decentralisation of power in practice turns into delegation of power. Delegation of powers means that prerogatives lie in the centre. But decentralisation of powers, on the other hand means diffusion of powers to the local institutions with least control from above. The policy of decentralisation of power is based on the fact that people have right to choose a system which they like most.

The very basis of rural life is the prevailing active co-operation among the villagers themselves. This co-operation can be further cemented and developed only through village Panchayats. So the Village Panchayat has a great responsibility of developing the Village and making the villagers able citizens of the century. So the Panchayat System, primarily based on village panchayats is the refined form of local self-government and the system's philosophical ideal is the consciousness of the common people of the country.

In the tides of the history of the world many countries rose to height and many powerful countries vanished from the scene. For some time the Divine Right Theory also virtually ruled over the people but the natural rights of people violently opposed it. Many philosophers like Machiavelli, Bodin Hobbes and Locke gave inspiration for the rise of events. But because of these incidents, a history of the world which comprises of success and failures of mankind has been written. The Panchayat System after crossing all these barriers has come to us. Inspite of all those great upheaveals the rural life of people remained intact. This is an obvious result of the then existing and also the present co-operation among the village folks. No system of government can be run well without enlisting an active participation for the state affairs from the villagers of that country. This has already been nicely proved by the history of the world. Sikander the great who had aspired for conquering the whole world, the Roman Empire which had dreamed of ruling the whole globe, the Czarist regime of Russia and the age old rule of the Britishers over India cannot be found now except in the pages of history. But villagers from a distant quarter had witnessed all these events. And in this 20th century the importance of villagers have increased tremendously and no democrative government can be run effectively without their active participation.

For a balanced development of a country both the government at the centre and the local institutions have to play an equally important role. The local government has a great responsibility of educating people of the country in order to make them able and dutiful citizens of the nation. In a country like Nepal village panchayats train future administrators of the country and simple rural folks can learn from these local institutions lessons about their rights and duties. Local people can learn much from village panchayats about the importance of election and that of their rights and duties than from a long preaching of an orator. So the Panchayat System which has been long cherished by the people and has root throughout the length and the breadth of the country is most likely to be a permanent and fruitful system of government in Nepal. So one can easily say that the measuring role of success of democracy is successful working of village panchayat and this success in turn depends on the development of the country and that of democracy. Thus one can conclude that the Panchayat System is the basic order designed to lay a firm foundation of democracy in the country.

Since the Panchayat System has developed out of the Nepalese soil as a part of people's thought, the Panchayat philosophy can also flourish well with the popular aspirations. In the parliamentary form of government philosophy tends to develop from above. But the defect of parliamentary government is characterised by total absence in the Panchayat System where there is always tendency to develop from below. Thus we can declare without any hesitation that the Panchayat System is based on a progressive political philosophy.

Nobody can give us a precise definition and way of administration of a true democratic system. The Panchayat System in fact tallies with the Nepalese historical tradition, social, political, and economic conditions and aspirations of people. The success of a system of government in a country, by far depends on its foundation. This statement actually fits in the Panchayat System in Nepal. And, since the system is a brilliant part of the Nepalese history; the system can also be called as an inner expression of the feelings of the people. Here it is important to recall the wise saying of His Majesty King Mahendra, the propounder of the Panchayat Philosophy that, "In our country surrounded by forests and rivers, development of culture and civilisation has also been attained under the Panchayat System." So it becomes crystal clear that fountains of the Panchayat-philosophy are the cultural heritage and traditions of the people.

The implementation of the Panchayat System in the country, the formulation of the constitution which is perfectly in line with the Panchayat System, the election of the Panchas and His Majesty's first address to the National Panchayat on Baisakh 5,2024, are the solid example of the fact that the Panchayat Philosophy has already been put into practice. And this successful implementation of the Panchayat System of government has posed a great historical challenge to the world. Time has also rightly testified that the Panchayat Philosophy is quite dynamic in nature.

After a deep study of 40 years of the Western capitalistic system, Karl Marx wrote his Communist Manifesto, in 1848. It was really the origin of the idea of socialism and political thinkers of the whole world paid due attention to it. And it was only in 1917 that after the Great Revolution in Russia that the idea of socialism was put into practice. But in Nepal within less than a period of 3 years the country, by discarding the Parliamentary System entered into a Panchayat area. It goes without saying that within that shortest possible time the

Panchayat System had already gained ground in the soil of the country. Thus the Panchayat System is based on the consciousness of the Nepalese people and future of the country depends on the very success of the System. In this way the Nepalese people with the Panchayat System have arrived in the threshold of a new era. Moreover the Panchayat philosophy is based on the experiences of Nepal; so it is an original political philosophy.

One of the foundation-stones of the Panchayati-Philosophy is the theory of common good. As a matter of practice commoners are more interested about their relatives. But a conscious man knows very well that welfare of an individual also comes within the general well-being of the society. For the successful working of democracy, a new line of thinking based on general welfare is absolutely necessary. This theory of common good is the foundation of the Panchayat democracy. In absence of this glowing spirit democracy cannot function well. And one of the ideals of the Panchayat System is to bestow upon individual a chance of choosing his representative without any compulsion. So the Panchayat System does not curtail individual liberty.

One of the speciality of the Panchayati-Political Philosophy is unity in diversity. According to the principles of decentralisation of powers all the village panchayats come within the jurisdiction of independent local self-government. They are both centres and the foundations of the Panchayat System. It is in the villages that the plants of democracy grow, and democratic ideas are diffused. Members of every Village Panchayat are free to implement works by the way they like most. In this sense there are many components within the country itself but the aim of the system is to bring unity in the midst of diversity. So the aim of the Panchayat Philosophy is to help strengthen national unity of the country. The Panchayat System has spirit of unifying the country by maintaining a harmonious relation among the various communities of the country. Since the Panchayati ideals are familiar to the people, it is through this system that the country can record a faster pace of development in various fields. Slogans are not sufficient for proper growth of a country; familarity of political ideology is more important for that. A proof of the fact that the Panchayat System is better than the parliamentary form of government is that within a shortest possible time of 3 years the former system has become successful enough in finding out its own way. The main political task of the day is to unite various intellectuals hitherto-divided into different groups. Mr. Harold J. Laski has nicely written that, "The ability to find out a new basis for unity then becomes the condition for the survival of parliament." This unity can be very well maintained in the partyless Panchayat System.

All subsequent events which took place in this world after the World War II proved beyond any body's doubt that democracy should be developed from the very beginning. In this proper background, the Panchayat System based on the life and tradition of the Nepalese people has been introduced in the country. The history of the world is a record of fighting between kings and peoples. But in Nepal the King gave leadership for the establishment of democracy in the country. So our system of government established by the co-operation of the King and people is different from the rest.

Although England is called the mother of parliamentary government yet the system is not entirely of her own. Not does the system of the government entirely belongs to France. Since parliamentary government contains features of the West it can be called a Western system. Although the Panchayat System is based on life and tradition of the Nepalese people yet it cannot be said a system belonging to Nepal alone. India has also a Panchayati heritage and so is the case with many other Asian countries. So the Panchayat System can better be called an Eastern System. In the Orient the Parliamentary from of government is gradually withering away and the Panchayati system is proving its usefulness.

The Panchayat is our own system of government, because it is not a carbon copy of others. It is a system developed in the country and familiar to its people. Here it is worth recalling the speech of His Majesty the King, "For an all round development of the country we have to find out a new source of strength which will do away with our country-old poverty, illiteracy, backwardness and help develop democracy suited to the conditions of the country. Since Panchayat System is the foundation of democracy and on the touch-stone of experience the democracy imposed from above has proved to be a failure, we have to strengthen the foundation of democracy from below. It is our aim to develop local self-government by making people to participate in Village Panchayat, Zilla Panchayat, Nagar Panchayat and in the affairs of the state. We have taken a firm conviction that those individuals who were hitherto indulged in different political parties will take part in this system." Under the parliamentary system the country experienced the rule of a few hands from the centre. But in the Panchayat System a provision has been made and that the problems of villages are solved by the trustworthy persons of the village through consent; the difficulties of city are met peacefully by the true representatives of city dwellers and similarly the inconvinences of Zilla and Anchals are discussed and solved by the trustworthy elected representatives of Zilla and Anchals."

All these sayings of His Majesty the King indicate that the Panchayat is the system which has divided the administrative responsibilities into different parts so that maximum popular participation may become a reality and that in this system every problem is solved through compromise. This in fact is an ideal of every form of democracy. And Nepal has adopted the panchayat system of government to realise this ideal. "The target of every association, institution, organisation, and that of ism is development. But it has become a common experience that in the absence of honesty the same institution or the ism becomes a hurdle for development of a country. Everybody knows that this is not only the experience of ours; many South—East Asian countries have also felt the same." All these sayings of His Majesty the King not only emphasise the importance of the Panchayat System; but also expose the fallacy parliamentary government. Both our means and end must be fair. Party democracy so far has not attained its goal fully.

His Majesty King Mahendra on the basis of history has

proved that there is a close relationship between the ideals of the Panchayat System and political process. The political process has been developed on the basis that, "no one may unduly exploit the others, rich may not have full and unjust away over the poor and every individual may be in a position to take part in administration." This is also the target of the Panchayat System. So from political view point one can say that the experience of the parliamentary system was an incident and the panchayat system is a political process. Although the ideals of the parliamentary form of government are also the same yet defects of the party system arise in the way of their realisation. So party system can better be called an incident of history than calling it a political process. The Panchayat System never condemns other form of governments and is always ready to derive merits from every other system. No body takes it had to learn good from others. The constitution of India has also taken good aspects of many constitutions of the world as Presidentship from the American constitution, Parliamentary system from England, Directive Elements from the Irish constitution and so on. Here it is worth remembering that the Panchayat system is not antinomos of parliamentary government, the former is only a refined form of the later. It is for the simple reason that the ideals of the Panchayat system and that of parliamentary government are identical only faces are different.

In the process of development parliamentary system and party system have almost become identical to one another. But the experiences of the Nepalese people tell them that political parties who see nothing except their own self-interests are a great hindrance to the proper development of a nationalistic feeling and cannot represent people adequately. In socialism proletariates lord over other classes of the society and the only political party turns into a dictator. In party system medium of mass communications are misutilised and thereafter public opinion is created, which is fragile and cannot represent a true public opinion. Under communism there is no multi party system and the party represents no one put itself. But the Panchayat System has choosen a path which is different from both the systems. The Panchayat System being partyless has no demerits of "party democracy" and "party dictatorship." In the Panchayat System one class can not rule over the other. People in Panchayat discuss their own problems and find a way out. Here for the healthy growth of public opinion door is opened for the expression of individual's view and for reaching at a solution. Party system could not deliver goods in underdeveloped countries. Although socialism assures a faster pace of economic development yet it is negation of human nature. Socialism has utterely neglected the spirit of class co-ordination and blindly follows the same principles again and again. But the panchayat system is wider than this. The original background of the Panchayat System are discussions and compromises. So the speciality of the Panchayat philosophy is that it does not hate other isms of the world. "In between parliamentary system and communism, existence of the Panchayat System is possible. Panchayat System largely represents public "and" if this system is not beneficial for us, let us have a frank exchange of views, I am prepared for this." All these sayings of His Majesty King Mahendra, the propounder of the Panchayat system, indicate a liberal approach of the order. Thus in a untshell the Panchayat System is more rational than communism or parliamentary government.

Democratic ideals crop up from village level. The basic requirement for successful working of democracy are political awakening and a sense of duty among the common people. These fundamental requisites are provided by village panchayats and it is in this sense that this sort of government it often called a "Basic Democratic System." The different tier of the local self-government, in the Panchayat System have been taken as an integral part of central government. The Panchayat System has become successful enough in maintaining a uniform pattern of administration right from top to bottom. It is because of this uniform pattern that the Panchayat System sometime seems to be a centralised government, but the very principle of this government is decentralisation of powers so it can better be called a centralisation. The followers of socialism also preach similar views, but they are foundamentally different from the one which we have got in the Panchayat System. The Panchayat System aims at the development of society on the basis of national unity and by providing individual rights. Thus the Panchayat System has established a dynamic relationship between individual and society. So in the Panchayati-philosophy there is a nice co-ordination between collectivism and individualism. In this system everybody feels that he is ruling himself and a sense of duty arises in his heart for furthering the tempo of development of the country.

An universally accepted democratic principle is that—"people have got right to govern themselves." But a large number of people can never solve their problems. So a system of choosing popular representatives to govern the people has come up. The representatives apart from being honest and dedicated must be in a position to safeguard the interest of common people well. For that the voters also must have an adequate knowledge about the integrity and talent of the representative whom he is going to vote for. It is but natural that nobody wants to vote for a person who does not know the voter's difficulty. Much depends on the mode of election.

Democratic government is not a new thing for this world. According to the learned men even in the old days of the governments of Mesopotemia, Mexico, Egypt, China etc, some elements of democratic ideas were present, but that was a direct but not a representative democracy. To day it is unimaginable to run a direct democracy, so people choose their own representatives. Success of democracy these days largely depends on these representatives. If the representatives are able a working democracy can be established in the country; otherwise the country is sure to ruin. Thus the first step of making nemocracy a success is holding of an election. It is in this sense that people say that election determines the future of a country. So in a democratic system every individual is given a chance of determining the future of the country. The first requisite of a democratic system is the holding of a free election.

In our country more than 97.18 per cent of population live in villages. The villagers know their difficulties well and can find a way out of it. A villager knows very well that his welfare is linked with the development of that village. He is well aware if his village cannot prosper he would be no where. So for him the village is the extension of his cottage. But the simple village folk cannot easily understand that the nation is also composed of many villages. We can also make it clear to the villagers that their fate is linked up with the village in which they live. But impartation of great education is necessary to make people conscious that their fate is invaribly liked up with the nation. So in a system where the villagers are entitiled to choose their representatives they select the one who can safeguard their interest. In a party system or under a parliamentary system people have to go far in order to elect their representatives. And in a society where a majority of people are educated and well-informed, and means of mass communications are fully developed people know merits and demerits of various candidates to a greater extent. But in a country like ours where the literacy figure does not go up more than 4.89 per cent and means of mass communications are least developed it is not possible for each and every villager to know at length the abilities of various candidates living in other parts of the country. Thus it is beyond anybody's doubt that only in a village-level election the voters can fully safeguard their interests. In a system of election where the people can know abilities of various candidates well, the voters can not be misled. In the absence of political parties in the Panchayat System the local people in the country can elect their representatives in an environment of peace, tranquility and better understanding. It is practical political reality of the Panchayat Political Philosophy.

The basic democracy of Pakistan has been framed on this line. Similarly no one can claim that Mahatma Gandhi, the foremost leader of the Indian Independence Movement by reading his ideology on Panchayatraj, say that he wholeheartedly had supported a parliamentary government. At a time when India attained her freedom it was generally accepted that parliamentary system was best for all countries. It was also a time when a wave of independence had swept over Asia and Africa and the fallacy of parliamentary system was not yet exposed. On one hand the successful stablishment of a socialist regime gave added impetus to establish similar form of governments in China, and Poland, while on the other hand the failure of parliamentary governments of Egypt, Pakistan, Burma and Indonesia proved futility of the system in an alien environment. So in the last decade the politics of world has changed. The views of Mahatma Gandhi on Panchayat prompt us to think that if he were alive and India had to achieve her independence in 1961 instead of in 1947 she also might have practised a Panchayat System. Gandhiji declared, "A group of 20-men from centre cannot run a democracy. For that every member of village panchayat must try from below . . . ." At a time when parliamentary system was supposed to be a successful form of government Gandhiji advocated for Panchayatraj. As a matter of fact Gandhiji's ideal form of government for India was the Panchayatraj; his opinion of parliamentary system was that it was a means to reach the goal of Panchayatraj. Mr. Joyti Prasad Suda, a well known writer of India says, "British institutions have been imitated by many nations, the difference is only of degree. They were thwarted on us because of our political dependency upon them." So all these analysis make it clear that Mahatma Gandhi and many other Indian people were in favour of the Panchayatraj and only an adverse circumstance compelled them to choose a parliamentary government. Mahatma Gandhi has emphatically stressed the need for choosing a form of government which can tally with conditions, culture, and heritage of that nation and help develop a pattern of society based on those ideals. Gandhiji vehemently criticised Panchayatraj run on party line. According to Mahatma Gandhi the magnaminity of the Panchayatraj lias in doing work on the principle of common good. It is really a practical political philosophy. Our Panchayat System is also based on all these practical realities. And if we compare to the works which the country could perform in 10 years (1950-51 to 1960) they stand far less satisfactory than the one which the nation has recorded in a three years period since the inception of the Panchayat System.

Dr. Radhakrishanan, the President of India has rightly remarked that, "We have to work from the bottom upwards, if any public discipline is to be maintained in our public life". The late Premier of India Shree Jawaharlal Nehru had also remarked. "The real foundations of freedom and democratic structure are being firmly laid by these movements. This is the real Swaraj of the people." The opinion of both the people on Panchayat are full of hard facts. The ideal of Mahatma Gandhi was a message of peace designed to uplift the Indian society above petty trifles like violence, personal rivalary and so on. If Gandhiji were alive to day he might have been pleased to see that his ideals have been well realised in this mountanious kingdom by the joint efforts of the King and the people. The Panchayat System adopted by Nepal is partyless and provision of the National Panchayat is also there. So in practice it is more scientific than the conception of Mahatma Gandhi's Panchayatraj. The Panchayatraj of Mahatma Gandhi is only an ideal whereas the Panchayat System of Nepal is a working political philosophy and in which all the elements of modern democratic principles are present. The Panchayat System has been adopted to meet the challenge of time. This is but a political reality."

By adopting the Panchayat System Nepal has also maintained her independence, it is because the system is quite natural to the country. For the proper development of an individual or that of society this spiritual independence is no less important than a political independence. Apart from this the Panchayat System is heading towards a fully developed democracy by adopting proper political and economic measures.

6

The Economy and the Panchayat System

"The Panchayat democracy is not merely a system of government, it also indicates a sound economic, political and social order." This wise saying of His Majesty King Mahendra, the propounder of the Panchayat System amply reveals that the Panchayat has followed a system peculiar to its own A full-fledged democracy has three aspects, economic, political and social. To a great extent the success and viability of a democractic system do depend on economic factors. Thus there, is a close kinship between economics and politics. Economic policies adopted by the Panchayat System is a different one, which in fact has become a co-ordinator between the fully state-owned socialist economy and that of capitalism where the capitalists have full sway over the country. Thus "class co-ordination" which has become the theoretical base for the Panchayat philosophy, is also its economic feature. In other words the Panchayat economy is developed and expanded by the help of haves and have-notes and capitalists and labourers. Actually speaking the Panchayat System is based on 'Panchaiti (discussion),' in turn whose main working philosophy is class coordination.

The happenings in Afro-Asia nations in their post-independent era have amply proved that without economic well-being of the people, political and social changes have little meaning. To achieve economic self-sufficiency in many parts of the world revolutionary measures were adopted and slogans mongered. But in Nepal with the co-operation of the King and People' revolutionary measures, in a peaceful way, have already been implemented. Nepal, today in comparision with many advanced countries, is lagging far behind yet she, in a planned way, has already made a good start. And the motive force behind the tempo is the policy of class—coordination so dearly cherished by the Panchayat System.

It may here be recalled that in Europe political and economic changes took place at one and the same time. To put the same thing in other words, in Europe economic and Industrial Revolution were contemporary to the political revolution. But in Asia the political change has preceded economic revolution, its whole impact was also felt by Nepal in 1950-51. In this way one can see a distinct difference between the political change which occurred in Europe and the one which took place in Asia.

Karl Marx, had always emphasised economic aspect of the society and working members had been inspired by the Industrial Revolution. His books by and large dealt with the outcomes of the Industrial Revolution and he imagined socialism under those evils. But the country which first adopted socialism was a primitive nation and the whole economy was heavily based on agriculture. So was the case with China, the great nation of Asia.

Since an overwhelming number of people in Nepal depend on agriculture for their livelyhood their standard of living is not sure to rise without corresponding development in agriculture. In order to change the prevailing system of land, people in some countries advocate communism while others socialism. Since the present set-up of democracy has failed in many parts of the world to solve the problem of the farmers, many a politician pleads for socialism. But in Nepal the need of a separate 'ism' did not arise because under the Panchayat System all the revolutionary measures have been implemented peacefully.

Under the present form of democracy the workers are not properly represented. Its obvious repereussion is the origination of the idea of dictatorship of the proletariates. But under the Panchayat system of democracy apart from other classes the peasants are also properly represented and the Land Reform measures have conferred tenancy rights on them, thus improving the lot of the tillers. It is the reflection of the fact that the Panchayati-economy is dynamic in nature. Hollow political slogans may lead to economic dependence. Thus in order to help strengthen political freedom economic development is a prime necessity, in which direction the Panchayat System is heading forward.

It is after the First World War that the idea of socialism gradually spread while after the Second War the need for changing the traditional economy was keenly felt. In many countries of the globe a number of progressive measures were introduced to get rid of the traditional economic system. Although a number of new philosophies regarding democracy are appearing yet the guiding factors are the same. So is the case with economic theories. So, it is but natural to give brith to an economic philosophy which suits the soil of a particular country. It was the economic revolution which had taken place in Germany that led to more production and also unequal distribution. This queer circumstance inspired Marx to give birth to a new philosophy. The dictum of Marx says that the gradual development of capitalism leads to communism. But in actual practice communism first took its root in underdeveloped Russia rather in developed England. America, France or Germany. This alone leads us to the conclusion that "it is not the industrial capitalism which leads to communism but that the underdeveloped economy itself invites the rein of the proletariates." Thus Mr. Ashok Mehata, the great socialist leader of India in his book Democratic Socialism has said, "Economic theories are the product of economic facts and economic situations which in turn are influenced by the emergence of new economic theories". Similar opinions have been expressed by a large number of economists. In a nutshell economic factors and economic environment can give birth to a new economic theory. It would be rather illogical if we rigidly try to uphold a given theory. England could well-develop herself in the absence of planning. And, with the successful implementation of planning in the Soviet Union other underdeveloped countries followed the same pattern. It is not the outcome of economic theory; it is a product of economic facts and environments which more often than not are influenced by the given conditions. Nepal, also realising all these facts, has adopted economic policies which completely tally with the economic facts.

The ingredient factors for economic development in an underdeveloped country are capital, planning and labour. The rate of economic growth can not be geared only shouting to end the capitalism. However, in the process of development one cannot leave capitalists with free hands for the fear being that such capitalists will be the backbone of exploiters thereby defeating the very purpose of democracy. So policy of the Panchayat system of democracy has been one of trying to strike a proper balance between the capitalists and the labourers. The Panchayat System aims at the minimisation of class conflict without giving a free hand to the prolertariates as in the case of communism, to govern the other classes of the society. The System, by exploiting its limited capital and other means has tried to derive a new economic system. The well-renowned economist and leader of India Mr. Ashok Mehata has pointed out three means of forming capital in an underdeveloped economy:

1. Traditional capitalist method—According to this programme the labourers are forcefully employed at a given work.
2. The second method is the one developed by Stalin—of forced collectivisation of agriculture and industrialisation through slave labour. Under this system those

people who voice against terrible strain are regarded as the enemy of the people and it also takes for granted the fact that the teeming millions are only raw materials.

3. The last way is to develop through the consent of the people. Under this system, for economic development people should devote their heart and soul. The labour is voluntarily achieved. This can also be called a democratic way.

For the economic development of Nepal we have got a vast resource of manpower. And this resource is gradually going to be utilised by the Panchayats through the consent of the people. It is a policy of class co-ordination which is the unique feature of the Panchayat democracy.

The main aim of the Panchayat System is to duly regard individual liberty and humanity—that is the reason why the Panchayat System has utterely disregarded the first two principles since they do not value those sacred objectives. The third tenet is democratic in nature and fits the Panchayat democracy. In an underdeveloped country like Nepal where manpower supply has its own importance any policy which is designed to exploit it through consent should receive wide applause.

Although Nepal is primarily an agricultural country—yet the agricultural tools are as good as primitive—the reason for this is not far to seek e.g. prevalance of feudal system of land ownership. So the land reform programme has been launched to do away with discrepancy existing between the owners and tillers so that the tenants could cultivate the land with still closer interest. "In a country like ours where agriculture has played an overwhelming role, economic development by and far depends in the development of agriculture and at our present condition industrial development is possible only by developing the agricultural sector."

The one and only way of preserving and protecting democracy and freedom in Afro-Asia is the fastest pace of economic development. Like a system of government little benefit can be derived by imitating any rule of development from others. The supporting fact for this statement is that every country has economic facts and conditions peculiar to others. We had already experienced the so-called capitalist form of economic development and that of the socialists. But our experiences guide us to the fact that both of them are an unmixed blessing. It is high time that both of them be changed to suit the need of time; as to Nepal she has already devised a different System. And in fact the Panchayat System has played that role by following an independent economic policy. This system has not only bridled the capitalist horse but the proletariates are also checked from having a sole voice in the economic matters of the state. It is thus a system devised to develop the country by the active co-operation of the capitalists and the labourers. Thus unique system can also be called a mixed economy. Under the Panchayat System thus neither the state has owned a full control over the factors of production nor the capitalists are given a free-hand. But this is not to say that the system has in any way curtailed individual liberty.

Like our system of government the economic policies are not also carbon copies of others. The Panchayat System has done well by extracting good of both capitalism and that of socialism. In this sense the Panchayat can properly be called a bridge between those two system. By not infringing individual liberty, land reforms and civil codes have been implemented which are by nature socialistic. Those reformations have been peacefully carried out and in root they have the blessing of the King. The true basis of these developments is the result of the existing cordial relations between the King and his subjects. A part and parcel of our history is that the Kings have always become the fountain of reformations. A large number of reformative measures which were even outside the dream of the so called socialist government like the new civil code and the land reform measures have been promulgated after the political change of 1960 which in effect have brought about social revolution. This is a substantial proof of the fact that the Panchayat is both a dynamic and a revolutionary system.

From another angle also the Panchayat economy seems to be different from the rest. The factor which separates capitalism from the rest is the recognition of "individual liberty" while the socialists are separated by the principle of "justice for all in distributing the sum total of production." But the Panchayat economic policy has adhered to the principle of individual rights and freedom. The target of the Panchayat System is the realisation of the concept of a welfare state. It aims at distributing the production by a socially justifiable way. During the days of Karl Marx, the originator of modern communism, in Germany, due to the industrial revolution production had recorded a high growth but the machinery of production were controlled by a few hands. The obvious result was that the commoners and the labourers alike could not enjoy the fruit of the development. Keeping this bitter fact in mind Marx upheld the conception of Socialism—for the achievement of social justice and economic liberation.

It is here needless to repeat that distribution follows production. The Panchayat System has given primary importance to production and only secondary to distribution. The system has also stressed the need for producing more both in the primary and secondary sectors. Really the increased production has to match with the rise in population without slackening the tempo of industrialisation. Thus our first need is the rise in production and equal attention is given to the fact that production should be distributed on the basis of social justice. In this way the Panchayat System has established a relation between the individual and the community. It has struck a golden balance between the collective and individual interests. This itself has helped much in realising the objective of the Panchayat System e.g. to prepare ground for such an environment where an individual could develop his personality to the fullest possible extent.

According to economic theory the key factors of production are the formation of capital, provision of transportation, manpower resources etc. All these factors can be well exploited only by implementing proper planning. Nepal has also followed the same track and has already completed her Three Year Plan by the end of last June is now implementing a Five Year Plan. The current plan has given top priority to agriculture and transportation. There is also a provision for industrialisation.

Learned men thought over the conception of democratic-socialism, but they themselves reached the conclusion that none can give correct nature of such a system. As against this under the Panchayat System the economic policies are controlled by democratic means. And this method of reformation is superior to that of reformations under socialism, the simple reason accountable for this being that under the Panchayat System there is individual liberty, a full-fledged chance bestowed upon the individual to develop his personality. It is but an established fact that free agriculture means independent people. "Collective farming and peoples' non-attachment to land are good examples to preach. But in practice they are hard to realise. Under collective farming the return which an individual is entitled to receive is constant irrespective of his efforts." Out of the total production both strong and weak, active and inactive receive in the same proportion." So in such a state of affairs there cannot be a co-ordination between the output and ths efforts. In contrast to this the Panchayat System has accepted individual ownership of land. This has given him adequate incentive. So he tills the land with his heart and soul. Under socialist form of government inspite of high-sounding slogans like "economic equality" and catch-words like the "dictatorship of proletariates" in practice the single party plays the role of an autocrat and an individual finds himself meaningless in such a society. Stalin himself had declared, "The proletariate cannot exercise power together with other classes e.g. the peasantry, and that dictatorship of the proletariate means Communist Party dictatorship." It will be quite sensative if we evaluate economic development by democratic measures rather than by seeing through the goggles of any 'ism'. It is natural that the process of development of country be guided by geographical, social, economic and historical factors. No economic system is without its shortcomings. The real cause being economic and social environments are ever changing: The settlement by nomads in a particular place and tilling a large tract of land by them was the historical revolution. Similarly the ownership of land which comprised big size was also a solid step towards economic development. Today any action which ends feudal exploitation and helps strengthen economic well-being is regarded all the more revolutionary practice. So there is a fundamental difference between the theory of economic development and that of pure science. Although the Panchayat System has taken good aspects of other systems yet it is a type of its own, quite dynamic in nature and modern in outlook.

There are two ways of developing a country :

1. The Reformative, and
2. Crisis and Catastrophy. Sometimes both the ways divert the target itself.

Those who uphold the theory of crisis and catastrophy do not even hesitate to break down the state machinery. Reformists visualise for changing the society through reforms. Panchayat System also votes for the reformative tendency—whose main ideal is to bring peaceful revolution in the society.

After the end of the last war almost all the countries affiliated themselves, directly or indirectly with the major international issues. This can be well visualised in Nepal also particularly when she became the member of the U.N. in 1956. After the political change of 1950 under the able and dynamic leadership of His Majesty the King, Nepal has been internationally well-known and a number of friendly countries including the U.N. and its allied agencies have made available economic assistance in a substantial amount. This assistance has become quite helpful in making the Nepalese economic self-sufficient one. In Nepal at present while on the one hand through the land reform measures agricultural sector is gradually developing and on other to raise the national income, to give works for the idle hands and to make the country self-sufficient industrial development is gaining ground. This is a sound proof of the fact that the Panchayat is a dynamic system.

The Industrial Revolution gave fresh impetus to capitalism to bloom to the fullest possible extent. Its obvious repercussion was the origin of the idea of socialism. But the first country where socialism came into practice was far from being developed. Since the techniques of production were also obsolete, there socialism slowly but gradually developed into a party dictatorship. So the supporters of socialism opine that, socialism can not be built in an underdeveloped economy." This leads us to the conclusion that a country cannot be a socialist by repeating word "Socialism" time and again. The economic policy adopted by the Panchayat System is neither socialist in nature nor capitalist in content; it is but a natural product of Nepal's economic condition and environment. The System is in no way impressed by any utopian 'ism'. It is a natural product of the soil. After 69 years of the origin of the idea of socialism in 1917 a socialist economy was established in the USSR. After that many a country followed the lead. But still in practice the shape of a socialist economy can not be described. The reason being there are socialists who want to adhere to democratic means and oppose dictatorial tendency. But the case of our Panchayat is altogether different. It has already adopted a philosophy and gradually going to realise in practice. Through the principle of decentralisation of powers, every layer of Panchayat is given social, economic, and a power to pursue an independent policy." In conclusion the economic aspect of the Panchayat System in as independent policy which is designed to achieve a self-generating stage. It is a policy of Industrialisation of the country through the development of agriculture.

All prerogatives which lie with 'His Majesty' have been designed to utilise in a constitutional way. "Whereas it is desirable in the best interest and for all-round progress of the Kingdom of Nepal and of the Nepalese people to conduct the government of the country in consonance with the popular will; "and" "Whereas the happiness and prosperity of Our beloved subjects have been always Our only objective for the accomplishment of which We are solemnly resolved"; This has been explicitly written in the preamble of the constitution of Nepal. And all these facts clearly prove that Nepal is a welfare state. "The main aims and objectives of the Panchayat System are to protect sovereignty, freedom, cultural heritage and glory of the past and also to create a partyless, pure and expliotation-less society. This speech of His Majesty the King all the more clarifies the fact that the aim of the Panchayat System is an establishment of a welfare state. It is a proud political achievement for Nepal. The freedom struggle was fought and democracy was established in the country for the Nepalese people and the aim of the Panchayat System is the consolidation of all these achievements.

It is an underlying fact that the aim of a revolution is to create a new society, where every person could feel secure and get opportunity to develop his personality. The speciality of the great revolution of 1960-61 of Nepal is that it has encouraged the Nepalese people to create a new and modern society. And the speciality of the Panchayat System under the able leadership of His Majesty King Mahendra is that the energy of the masses has been concentrated in the task of building up of a welfare state.

The main obstacles before us are the inequality and various social injustices. The Panchayat System aims at removing all these evils and has made broad a basis for attaining the ideals of welfare state. History says us. "The aim of the revolution of 1950-51 was only a revolution and no solid step was taken to create a new order in the society." So it becomes clear that the present government is more democratic than all the previous party-governments. It is a clearcut answer for those who say that with the end of the parliamentary system democracy also died in Nepal.

Every body can answer that democracy is a representative government. And the Panchayat System has also been fully supported by the people—the election and the establishment of the supreme legislative body, that is Rashtriya Panchayat (national panchayat) is a solid example of this fact. Moreover it was the active support extended by the people which has enabled this system to implement a number of progressive measures which the party government had never dream of doing that.

So in conclusion one can fairly remark that parliamentary government is not only a democratic government and at times a large number of reforms of which the Westminster type of governments had failed to carry on can be successfully implemented under the Panchayat System. The amount of success achieved by Nepal under the Panchayat System in such a brief period is a sound proof of the fact that the Panchayat is the best system of government for the country and its people. Here it is worth recalling the remarks of His Majesty the King, the propounder of the Panchayat System, "The Panchayat System is not a charity of any individual it is a system determined by history on the basis of material and other grounds."

The Social policy of the Panchayat System of democracy has been the establishment of a peaceful and exploitationless society. And the present Panchayati society has been divided into various class—organisations. And the solid basis of these class organisations is the principle of co-existence.

In theory, under parliamentary form of government various political parties do safeguard interest of people. It is said that in government various political parties do represent people. And origin of political party has also been to represent divergent interests of people. Thus the well known scialist leader, Stalin had remarked that, in socialism there is only one political party because there is only one class. In that classless society there cannot be a room for various political parties. "But even in a society where there are many classes their interests can be safeguarded even in absence of political parties; and even when there is no political party there can be democracy." It is really incorrect to say that only political parties can and do repesent class interests. The critics of party—democracy point out that no political party does represent the interest of the working class. A long history of party politics has alone substantially proved the criticism. Thus in the Panchayat System the interest of various classes has been properly safeguarded by different class organisations.

Every body has accepted the existence of various classes in society. Even in old days, society was divided into different classes. Really speaking the world has been created along with divergent groups. The reason behind the division is for work. It is the custom inherited from days immemorial. There are people who argue that the cause of the dlvision is economic. Some people accepted it into and rejected the existence of other classes vehementaly. But rationally speaking we cannot see the whole thing from economic view point alone. The division has been made on the basis of work for instance the work of teacher is to teach his pupils and the duty of students is to read. So we find various divisions in society which are other than economic.

Hegel and Marx have also divided classes on ground of works. But Marx gave more importance to economic factor. According to Karl Marx economic progress of a society has always been balanced by class conflict and strife. In this way one can read a narrow feeling of Karl Marx and his utopia of a classless society where exploiters and exploitees are characterised by their total absence. But to achieve this aim there is no need of establishing a socialist or a communistic state. Nepal under the Panchayat System is marching forward to a society which is free from exploitation. In communistic state of today which aims at attaining the ideals of Marx, there are many strong classes of army, businessmen, peasants and rulers and these classes gradually getting stronger. So Marx's conception of a classless society has turned into a class predominating society.

As a matter of fact the conception of classless society is against human society. A man in society cannot perform all works. So class division on the basis of works is an absolute necessary. And development of a society is possible only by striking a golden balance among various classess of a society. The conception of Marx's classless society is out of practice. And it has also been felt by all that in Marx's socialism party dicatorship is gaining firmer ground So the theory of class conflict which Marx assumed was an accident and class coordination is a process.

In ancient Hindu society also division was made on the basis of works. In Shirmad Bhagavat Gita also it has been written that "On the basis of merits and works the society has been divided into four classes." Even the basis of division made in the ancient Greek city state was on works. According to historians in the begining of creation there was no class in society. But in the process of development the society was divided after wards.

Thus the concept of class organisation developed with the development of the society. Therefore the concept of classless society is unreal and unhistorical.

War is not the means of development and conflict does lead us no where. Man is the witness of the fact that the First World War ended with aeroplane and the Second World war with atomic weapons. If the war monger's design of the Third War is realised that the whole universe will be turned into ashes. The number of the casualties of the First World War were—8 million killed and 19 million wounded. In the Second World War more than 15 million were killed and 5.5 million wounded. Apart from this about 10 million civilians were either killed or injured. The number of refugees also exceeded 10 million in all.

So the real basis for development of the world is peaceful—existence and the Panchayat system is also based on class co-ordination. And diffused form of this principle is universal brotherhood of mankind and peaceful co-existence. This also enables us to guess about the foreign policy of the Panchayat System. Nepal, to day under the Panchayat System of democracy is heading towards a society which is free from exploitation. But the basis of the proposed society is class co-operation. We do not advocate for class struggle. Our policy is not the climination of the rich people for the poor section of the community. Our target has been the creation of a classless society with the active eo-operation of the rich and the poor and for the benefit of both the classes. It is a feature unique to the Panchayat System.

As a matter of fact the concept of classless society is against the very way of thinking of human society. A society must be divided on the basis of works. In a society some people should be soldiers, some rulers, other farmers and so on. And it is in this way that class division on the basis of works must be acceptable to all.

Following are the names of various class organisations formed under the Panchayat System of government:

1. Nepal Peasants organisation.
2. Nepal Youth Organisation.
3. Nepal Women's organisation.
4. Nepal Labour Organisation.
5. Nepal ex-military men's Organisations.

Progress of a society is possible only when all these classes of society co-operate among themselves.

All these classes of society are formed under the Constitution. Thus one can readily admit the Constitution has duly recognised the importance of these various classes. The importance of these class organisations lies in proper development of mentality of various members of the society and in maintaing a cordial relation among them. People can freely work inside these organisations and it is also through these organisations that one can reach to the parliament of the people—the Rastriya Panchayat.

Even in party system there is a possibility for the existence of various class organisations. But in party system, party interest is stressed more than class interest. Similarly people of same interest, under party influence, join different political parties. The history of Nepal before 1960 shows that, "political leaders even in the slightest pretext of differences of opinion gave birth to a new political party and their only aim was to reach the height of power." Political parties were divided into groups. Almost every political party had its own parelled party.

To be leftist was supposed to be more progressive. Its impact was felt even by class organisations. But under the Panchayat System, people in the absence of self-dividing political parties can work on the principle of co-operation and co-existence. It is the speciality of the Panchayati class-organisations.

The very basis of the Panchayat System is mutual co-operation and the task of the various class organisations have been the uplift of their respective class and to enough of maintain unity among people.

In parliamentary form of government, even people of one class were divided into different groups or parties and engaged in the task of constant fighting. In the same fashion, being badly influenced by the then existing political parties, people of various classes fought against each other. This sort of fighting is not possible under the Panchayat System of Government. So the main task of the various class organisations has been promotion of good-will among the members of the various class-organisations in order to facilitate the national development.

From last many years political parties are representing people and ruling governments. But the time has changed and some sort of improvement is to be brought in this system. Party system of government in some parts of the world has divided popular force and led to a condition of constant struggle while in others it has given rise to party-dictatorship. But the history of emerging nations of Asia and Africa has shows that these party elements do not help develop nations. Even in the heginning of the 20th. century the party system was regarded as the best form of government. The salient feature of the twenteith century world is the rise of the idea of nationality and freedom among Afro-Asian nations. The last twenty years have considerably diminished the importance of party—politics and the political thinkers are thinking for alternative. Nepal had also to suffer much under the party system, and taking lesson from that she has adopted a partyless system of government. The argument put forward in favour of party system is that it alerts people and represents various interest. But in England, since there is no different interest of landlords and farmers there is no separate party of peasants. As a matter of fact political parties are supposed as a medium which represents the interest of people in government. But if Panchayats and class organisations represent interest of people in government there is no need of political parties. It is for this reason that class organisations have their importance in the Panchayat System. The class organisations have great tasks of training people in order to make them able to take part in the administration of the country and maintain good relation between Panchayats and themselves. The class organisations have to shoulder the important task of making people vigilant. The class organisations being alternative of different political parties must be in a position to make clear the people about the importance of self-government. So the class organisations have become the guard of democracy. The great deeds of class organisations are to safeguard the interest of their own class, of the nation and maintain cordial relation among different class organisations. All these facts show the importance of the class organisations in the Panchayat system of government.

As night has magnified importance of day or as trouble has increased importance of happiness similarly the theory of class struggle has intensified the importance of class co-ordination. To put the same thing in other words, the idea, the history and the experience of the theory of class struggle has increased the policy of class co-ordination. So it is necessary to deal with the theory of harmonisation of different classes at some length.

Marx was the first person who said that the development of human being has been made possible by dilectical materialism. According to Karl Marx the reason behind any political, social and economic changes is class conflict. According to him there are two underlying factors of a given society, (a) material forces of production, (b) and knowledge necessary to their use. These two factors create proper condition of production. There are two classes who can exploite this opportunity—the capitalists who are always engaged in the task of safeguarding their private fortune and a large number of labourers. In a capitalist economy the interest of labourers is utterly neglected. This condition leads to disharmony of relation between capitalists and labourers; and in turn this gives rise the idea of revolution in minds of workers. This is the beginning of the class conflict, And this disharmony of relation at last turns out to be class-warfare. So the essence of Marx's idea of class-conflict is a clash between the people who own means of production and the new ones who are gradually acquiring the tools of production. Those people who could benefit from the old relation has been called exploiters and the people who benefit themselves from new relation exploitees. Marx had a firm opinion that every society is divided by oppressors and oppressed. The history of all hihter to existing societies is the history of class struggle. State is also a part of class-struggle. State is an organised oppression. Thus Marx concludes that revolution is inevitable. Engels tells us, Marx reached the conclusion that at any rate, "inevitable revolution might be effected entirely by peaceful means" In later period of his life Marx was influenced by peaceful revolution of England. Earlier he had great confidence in this theory, like the law of gravity.

We can visualise the imprint of time in the Marxian principles. Analysing it in detail, the well-known socialist leader of India, Mr. Ashok Mehta points out that the Czarist Russia had greatly influenced the lives of Lenin, Trotasky and Stalin. In the regime, where they were brought up there was nothing like rights; they became anti-state. So Lenin came to the opinion that state is also a class dicatorship. The state being dictator rejects the rights of working class. It is a clear reflection of the idea of the time in which he was born. This is what he had experienced in his life. But his conclusion is unhistorical. Any society can be judged by rights and facilities offered to the working class. Even in highly capitalistic society of the USA and the United Kingdom rights of labourer have not been denied. There are many peasants and labour organisations who protect the interest of their class. To day, in a socialist economy and under party dictatorship if a man of peasant can be a minister of state so is true in Nepal. Thus one can fairly conclude that the outcome of the theory of class struggle was accidental not inevitable.

The essence of Lenin's theory is "Diamond cuts diamond." To put the same thing in other words. Lenin says that since the nature of state is class-dictatorship, it can be weeded out only by the force of the working class distatorship. But it is highly unrealistic to think an ultimate end of the state and form the concept of classless society.

The Paris Commune held in 1871 reckoned Karl Marx to think over a new principle. But the outcome of the Commune was that 20,000 were killed and about 140,000 were imprisoned. According to socialists this Commune became a model piece of proletariate and bourgeoisie class antagonism. And this led Marx to introduce some changes in his Communist Manifiesto. He emphatically pointed out that "the have nots can not easily control state machinery to achieve their ends." This amply proves that the theory of class struggle had come out of chance rather than from reality. Like Lenin Marx was not also unimpressed by his contemporary incidents. So we can accept the theory of class struggle not as universal fact but as an exception.

The main aim behind the socialistic way of thinking is to change the existing order in such a way that equality and justice prevails and exploitation comes to an end for ever. One can label any brand to that social transformation as one likes, but in a positive state all these can be achieved by peaceful means. Marx thought over his new principle being guided of the conditions of Germany. And Lenin was influenced by special happenings of Russia. Man from time immemorial is thriving and has recorded all sorts of developments. By accepting class struggle as the basis of progress, Marx has thrown a new light in history. Marx had propounded the theory of class struggle and socialism being influenced by the happenings of Germany and England aftermath industrialisation. But the first socialist nation was Russia neither Germany nor Britain. Progress achieved by Russia, in the first fourty years of socialist regime show that the achievements were due to class co-operation rather than struggle. And all class organisations who are supposed to be part of the state are growing stronger. Whatever it may be in principle, the socialistic history of the world has proved beyond any shadow of doubt that the establishment of a classless society is virtually impossible. So the historical or factual truth is that, "In a society there are various classes. And the conception of a classless society is untrue. The only way of progress is co-operation among the various members of the society."

Mr. Ashok Mehta, the well known socialist leader has pointed out that, only a positive state can be a socialist state. It is really an important thing for those persons who favour class struggle and classless society. The attitude of the Panchayat System in Nepal is positive. Here are separate entity of the various class organisations. Even peasants do represent in government. Each and every class of the society has been duly recognised. And all these classes have determined to change the cxisting condition of the country.

The present day world wide slogan of peaceful co-existence is in fact a magnified form of class co-operation. The way of thinking behind it is that the prosperity of mankind is possible through the co-operation of all the nations of the world. Since the concept of class co-operation is the basic fact of mankind, the Panchayat System of Government based on this policy is real, progressive and humanitarian.

In Nepal under the Panchayat System and on the basis of harmonisation of classes a great step has been taken for the development of the society. All these things are implemented even in the absence of socialist slogans and socialist parties. It is on the basis of class co-ordination that the Land Reform programme and Mulki Ain (new civil code) have been implemented. This Mulki Ain has done away with social inequality based on flimsy ground of sex or caste. The social policy of Panchayat System is to minimise the gulf existing between rich and poor, to eradicate overlordism of rich over poor, to create an atmosphere of understanding among the various groups of the country and to put an end of exploitation.

The constitution of 2019, Part 4 section (1) reads the aim of the state shall be to promote the welfare of the people by securing and protecting a just social order which bringe about harmony in the national life by integrating and consolidating interests of different classes and professions from a comprehensive national outlook." "Thus the supreme law of the land clearly declares the aims of the Panchayat System, and boldly puts forward social policies.

All political philosophies have their own separate policies on economic, social and political matters. If we turn the pages of the world history we come to the conclusion that whenever and wherever parliamentary government fails, communism in the name of the economic reconstruction of the country raises its head. But the aim of the Panchayat System is to create a free society based on the spirit of democracy. A backward country has always proved to be fertile ground for communism. The Panchayat System has already undertaken a number of progressive measures for the development of the country.

The Panchayat System has comphasised industrialisation of the country on the ground that in the absence of economic development democracy has little meaning and that political independence cannot stand in absence of a viable economic base. The land reform programmes help industrialise the nation.

These reforms are in no way inferior to the socalled socialistic reforms. As a matter of fact, all these reformative workings are more progressive than the socalled socialistic reforms, for reasons that we recognise individual's rights and they are implemented in a democratic peaceful way. Thus the Panchayat System has stressed very much the need of economic development on the valid assumption that political democracy in absence of proper economic backing is meaningless.

The past history of party politics has increased all the more the importance and the reponsibility to difference class organisations. Socialists have recognised class conflict as an important part of society whereas party politics promotes an open fire between the members of the same class. Thus under party system people of the same class interest or even of the same village join different political parties. Each political party proclaims their own policy and try to prove that it is better than of their opponents. It is only a part of their wish to reach in govt. by any means. In such a mess situation fight among the people of same interest group becomes inevitable. The Nepalese people experienced all these difficulties in the days of party—politics in Nepal. So the main task of the class organisations in Nepal have been to safeguard the interest of their own class, avoid class antagonism and create a proper background for an all round development of the country. The class organisations again have to create the feeling among the people that the every Nepali can contribute for the cause of national upliftment from their own seat. Every Nepali below the flag of class organisation can help develop the country.

Land reform programme has been regarded as modern, progressive and socialistic in nature. All Asian nations to day have recognised land reform programme as the step of economic revolution. Many nations of South East Asia like India, Pakistan, Burma and Indonesia are on the way of development by implementing their own way of land reform programmes. In some parts of the world land reform programme has been implemented by banishing landlords and compelling peasants to follow it. But in Nepal, under the Panchayat System of government the question of eliminating one class at the cost of the other does not arise at all. In this reference it is worth recalling the saying of His Majesty King Mahendra, "The Land Reform programme has not been implemented to benefit one class at the cost of other. Its basis is not class-conflict, it is class co-ordination. Thus one can say that if the principle of class coflict is the feature of the socialist regime, the theory and practice of class-co-ordination is the salient feature of the Panchayat System. Moreover the aim of the Panchayat System is to make people active in the tasks of national development. "The main ideals of the Panchayat System are to fulfil the wishes of the people, to uplift their economic condition, to safeguard people's political and social rights, to help develop a habit of mutual consultations among people, to make a nice provision of education for both the children of rich and poor alike, to protect people from exploitation by any political party or social groups or individuals, to run government according to sweet-will of people and to decentralise powers." These words of His Majesty the King, the propounder of the Panchayat Philosophy amply reveal the social, the political and the economic aspect of the Panchayat System.

The universal aspect of class-coordination is the concept of 'Peaceful Coexistence.' It is the way of thinking which visualises that peace and progress of mankind is possible only through co-operation and not coflict. It is because of this co-operation that the progress of the mankind has become possible. "The guiding principle of our foreign relation is an establishment of friendly relation with all the nations of the world". So the theory of class organisations which the Panchayat System has assumed on the basis of social organisations is a fact based on hard reality.

Change and Continuity

The Drama that the Himalayan kingdom witnessed on 15 December 1960 had not been written overnight. Silently and with infinite patience, the making of it had been spread over almost a decade. It might well be said that its writing started with the proclamation King Tribhuvan issued on his return to the kingdom. A grateful and joyous people acclaimed the King as their liberator, and the King thanked the people for their splendid endeavour to liberate as much the land as its sovereign. King Tribhuvan declared that "it is now our desire and our resolve that our people should henceforth be governed according to the provisions of a democratic constitution as framed by a constituent assembly elected by them. Until such a constitution is framed there should be a Council of Ministers, including representatives enjoying the confidence of our people, to aid and advise us in the exercise of our frontiers (with) our trusted and well-beloved Maharaja Mohan Shumsher Jung Bahadur Rana as our Prime Minister."

Every Nepalese man, woman and child was given to understand that a big change had taken place in the country in the months that had elapsed between the King's flight under duress to India and his triumphal return. The old order had crumbled in this short time, giving way to what promised to transform the country from being a mere object of history into its subject. The promise was the upland of peace, progress and prosperity, which was for the people to fulfil. Nothing stood between them and a smiling future but their own determination and judgment. Nepal belonged to its people and there was no going back on this, the men who had ridden the storm reassured them. But there was a wide gulf between the world of appearance and that of reality.

The most important aspect of the 1950-51 struggle was that it ended on a note of complete victory for one of the three parties to it, the monarchy. As for the other two—the people, as represented by the Nepali Congress, and the Ranas—it ended on a note of neither total triumph nor total defeat. The Nepali Congress gained partly what it had fought for, and the Ranas retained a share of the power they had enjoyed for about a century. For them the 1950-51 revolution ended on a note of compromise. The "Delhi formula" which eventually brought peace to all concerned was not a revolutionary document. It was not a written compact between the three parties to the struggle either. The author's interview with B.P. Koirala, reproduced here, throws light on the matter.

Q. You will perhaps agree with me that the 1950-51 revolution seemed to have been prevented from following its own logic by what has come to be known as the 1951 Delhi agreement, the three parties to which were the Nepali Congress, King Tribhuvan and the Ranas. What is your opinion about that, keeping in view the fact that not a few of your friends, particularly Rammanohar Lohia, the Indian Socialist leader, were strongly against your acceptance of the Delhi agreement at a time when the Nepali Congress was almost within sight of total success ? In other words, when the Nepali Congress, if it had not been restrained by the Delhi agreement, was posed for making a clean sweep of every impediment that stood in the way of transforming Nepal into a republic.

A. Bhola, there appears to be a general misconception about the compromise talks the three parties, namely the Nepali Congress, the King and the Rana, had in Delhi in 1951. In the first place, there was no regular agreement in the sense that the talks did not produce any document nor any papers signed on behalf of the three parties concerned. As a matter of fact, there was not even a regular conference. We did not sit together in any conference. The talks were conducted indirectly through the Government of India, whose good offices had been utilised to conduct the negotiations for the conference. I did not like this indirect method of conducting an important negotiation. But others, including my colleagues in the Nepali Congress, had different ideas. Ultimately, an understanding was reached basically on the following lines:

(*i*) King Tribhuvan would return to Kathmandu as King of Nepal.

(*ii*) His first act on his return would be to issue a royal proclamation pledging his word for a democratic constitution which would be framed by a constituent assembly elected on the basis of adult franchise. So far as I was concerned, I considered this point in the understanding as the most important achievement of the negotiation.

(*iii*) An interim government would be installed immediately after the King's return to Nepal. The interim government would be a coalition government of two equal blocs, that is, the Rana bloc and the Congress bloc. Mohan Shumsher Rana would continue to be Prime Minister. There was an understanding on the allocation of the portfolios in the Cabinet, which would have a strength of ten.

The second part of your question is: Whether or not it was possible for us to reject these terms and continue to fight as advised by Lohia. I personally was in favour of continuing the armed struggle; but I was in a minority in my party. The question that was discussed in the conference of the regional leaders of our fighting force along with the members of our

Working Committee, which met at Patna prior to our participation in the Delhi talks, was whether it would be possible for us to continue the struggle when the King and the Ranas and the Government of India were in favour of a compromise, In the event of our rejection of the proposal for a coference we would have to extend our struggle. It would have meant that we should even be prepared to fight the King and India. Tnis was considered a suicidal policy, however heroic it might have appeared to the people."

When the 1950-51 struggle was launched, the Nepali Congress had declared its objective was the establishment of a democratic socialist society in Nepal. But the struggle ended in a compromise, thus denying the Congress the condition precedent to fulfilling it pledge to the people. The very minimum the party had asked for was a place from where it could put its ideals into practice, but the way the struggle ended made it clear that it was not to be allowed to control the commanding heights of the polity. In the given context, the Nepali Congress had perforce to agree to function under a system that was farthest from what the armed sttuggle had apparently been waged to achieve. The struggle ended rather tamely and the leaders of yesterday's revolution had perforce to make the best of a had bargain.

History, circumstances and the party's own failings had as it were conspired to reduce the men who raised the standard of revolt to mere onlookers of a play that was staged far away from the sequestered valley of Kathmandu. It was New Delhi which alone could determine what should or should not happen in Nepal. And New Delhi had ideas that were materially different from the Nepali Congress thinking on the kind of policy the kingdom should have Prime Minister Nehru had outlined this before the Nepali Congress embarked on the struggle. "We have tried to find a way, a middle way, if you like, which will ensure the progress of Nepal and the introduction of or some advance towards democracy in Nepal. We have searched for a way which would, at the same time, avoid the total uprooting of the ancient order."

Of course it would not do to accuse New Delhi of having acted in bad faith. The Government of India, it ought to be recalled, was not a party to the goings-on in Nepal after freedom came to a partitioned subcontinent. Britain's withdrawal from the scene initiated its search for a "Himalayan policy," which for a number of reasons remained rather perfunctory. The critics of the government had harsh words to say and they charged it with neglect of one of the country's most vital aspects of security. Especially since China's emergence as a communist state had qualitatively altered the power in the region. The general drift of opinion was that the Himalayas had ceased to be the "traditional sentinel" which kept watch on the frozen northern heights which stood between the Ganga and the Yangtse King As Lohia, one of the most trenchant and consistent critic of the government's internal and external policies, put it," neither the snows nor the unscalable heights of the Himalayas can now do sentry duty for India. Contentment to the body and anchor to the mind of these 800 million people [who dwelt on either side of the southern Himalayan region] alone can provide security to India. Old concepts of foreign and defence policies must change. . .India, her people as well as her government, must evolve a Himalayan policy, which is both strategic and moral. . . The Indian Government has no policies." That criticism became much sharper after China's occupation of Tibet.

The appearance of Chinese troops on the Tibetan borders adjoining Nepal, Bhutan and Sikkim was not without its impact on New Delhi, however. Even prior to this the Government of India, as the successor state to the former British regime in the subcontinent, had concluded with Nepal two treaties of peace and friendship and of trade and commerce respectively in 1950. The peace and friendship treaty was not a mere exercise in polite diplomacy. Apart from what it publicly stipulated, the letters of exchange appended to the treaty—these were made public in 1959—enjoined: "Neither governmant shall tolerate any threat to the security of the other by a foreign aggressor. To deal with any such threat the two governments shall consult with each other and devise counter-measures."

New Delhi felt that the situation in Nepal could not be allowed to drift, aware as it was of the character of the Rana regime and the prevailing state of political uncertainties that only accentuated the growing discontent of the people. The distance between this and the argument for doing something positive, and without delay, to ensure that the Chinese presence remained restricted to the other side of the Himalayas was short. A friendly and reasonably stable democratic political system in Nepal was imperative if the Chinese influence, other things apart, was to be contained. The scenario up north was too arresting to be made light of.

Conceivably, this argument, besides ideological considerations, weighed with the Government of India in making things relatively easy for the Nepali Congress to operate from Indian soil. Circumstantial evidence would at the same time suggest that New Delhi limited the volume of assistance to the Nepali Congress to the extent that it would be obliged to stay moored to the concept of the "middle way." The guiding motivation of New Delhi was to have Nepalese politics restructured in a manner that would not thwart the eventual emergence of Nepal as a democratic polity. But nothing should be done which might at that point basically alter the relation of forces in the Himalayan kingdom.

Lohia's analysis and assessment of the policy New Delhi pursued was well within the bounds of logic. The developments immediately before and after the Nepalese revolution would not substantially invalidate his argument that the Indian government did not commit itself to a system of polity in Nepal that would enable the Nepali Congress to achieve the goal it had publicly pledged itself to. It is just that Lohia raised a very pertinent question but did not go into the reasons that determined the issue. If Nehru had been prepared to make B.P. Koirala his Douglas MacArthur in Nepal, he could decide in favour of a complete break with the past. The focus would necessarily have been on agrarian revolution. That was not to be. For India itself did not have its agrarian revolution, the bedrock of a democratic superstructure. To expect that India, which also did not make a "sudden break" with the past when it attained freedom, would work for a revolutionary solution for the problem of Nepalese politics would be asking for the impossible.

Nehru had left none in any doubt about the Indian government's thinking on the issue. All along he had emphasised that there must be no instant snapping of every link with the past. Time and again it was given out that the problem of Nepalese polity would have to be solved on the basis of compromise and understanding between the contending forces. The stress was on a middle way, between the old order and the ideal the Nepal Congress had inscribed on its banner—the demolition of the very basis of that society that had sustained the Rana regime for about a century. This was its *raison d'etre*. It was this that had prompted the party to take to armed struggle. That being the general belief, it shocked and surprised both friends and foes when the Nepali Congress agreed to work the Delhi compromise. But the apparent would not fully explain the Nepali Congress stand.

New Delhi had made a more or less objective appraisal of the Congress. There is no reason to believe that it was not aware of the Congress efforts to strive for a compromise with Mohan Shumsher before the struggle. This B.P. Koirala might be relied upon to vouch for. Along with Krishna Prasad Upadhyay, a Nepali Congress leader who became Speaker of the country's first elected Parliament, Koirala went to Kathmandu with the idea of negotiating a compromise with Mohan Shumsher. The mission failed without any dialogue between the Nepali Congress and the Ranas.

On this point let B.P. Koirala speak: "Perhaps. I project the image of a violent man. But, essentially. I am a peaceful person. Even when we were preparing to start an armed insurrection movement in Nepal, in 1948, I wanted to come to some kind of a settlement with . . . Maharaja Mohan Shumsher, so that an armed conflict might be avoided . . . I then went incognito to Kathmandu, and I wanted to contact him. I did not have any direct source. I thought the Indian Ambassador, Majithia . . . a great friend of the Rana family . . . might be of some help. I contacted the Indian Ambassador and told him what I wanted to do, that is, contact the Maharaja . . . He said that it was not possible for him to be the *via media* because that was not a job to be diplomatically performed. Then I approached a friend of mine who happened to be a tutor of Bijay Shumsher's sons, the grandsons of Mohan Shumsher, to contact Bijay Shumsher and tell him that we were preparing for an armed insurrection, that before the armed insurrection was launched I wanted to meet the Prime Minister and that our demands were very modest in that we should be permitted to organise political parties. The Ranas might rule the country but we must be free to organise political parties. My friend undertook the job and contacted Bijay Shumsher . . . and he communicated it to his father. But Mohan Shumsher was adamant. He said: No compromise. If he wants to meet me he should apply for an interview and write a *binti patra,* a prayer letter . . . 'When I decided to meet him it was not as a supplicant, I wanted to talk to him on equal terms. I was going to negotiate with him. I could not meet him on his dishonourable terms. I was living in Nepal incognito, and after a few days I was arrested."

This does not suggest that the Nepali Congress leader was agreeable to meet Mohan Shumsher on his terms and sign on the dotted line. At the same time the Nepali Congress leader had not even to the last day slammed the door to an agreement with Mohan Shumsher. It is a safe guess that such an agreement would not at any rate have been an improvement on the Delhi agreement.

Not much inside knowledge is necessary to appreciate that the Delhi agreement left the Nepali Congress high and day. The party had, for one thing, set off a revolution of rising aspirations. For another, confronted as it was by other political forces, including the Communists, it had perforce to maintain an image of militant radicalism and change. It also had to live up to its heritage of having led the revolution and its commitment to a reasonably changeoriented policy and programme. But that was far from the impression, which for one reason or another gained currency, that it was uncompromisingly committed to an immediate and radical change of the socio-economic fabric of society. It was not. Even some of its Socialist friends, for instance Jayaprakash Narayan, did not discourage it from accepting the Delhi agreement.

The formation of the post-revolution Cabinet with former Rana chief Mohan Shumsher as Prime Minister and B.P. Koirala as Home Minister, though a contradiction in terms to not a few, sharply outlined the emerging regime's political and class character. Koirala, whatever his public posture, which at any rate was not intemperate and which did not reflect any of the concern that some of his more obstreperous friends and colleagues had expressed, was not at all chary of working the compromise. He did not accuse Nehru of double standards or double talk. Instead, he granted that the Indian Prime Minister was one of the most straightforward and courageous men in politics. The most persuasive argument with Nehru, so far as his approach to Nepalese politics was concerned was that any drastic surgery on Nepalese society would create problems far too complicated for the Nepali Congress to handle. At another level it would inevitably involve India more directly and deeply in Nepal's internal affairs.

In the given context this would do good neither to India nor to the Nepali Congress. It would cramp the style of the Nepali Congress, apart from getting it branded as an echo of India's voice. The situation was one that did not enable the Nepali Congress to start from scratch. Then there was the King, who might not agree with the Nepali Congress scheme of things and might resent intensely his transformation from being a prisoner of the Ranas into a tool of the Nepali Congress.

Therefore, Nehru suggested, the Nepali Congress must have patience. It must work from within to get rid of the feudal setup and in this battle, as in the armed struggle, they must enlist the support of the King What Nehru told J.P. later may be recalled. As J.P. put it. "I remember Jawaharlal Nehru saying to me that . . . both are necessary for Nepal to exist and to prosper, both the monarchy and democracy as represented by the Nepali Congress today. It may be some other party tomorrow. But the people and the King both are essential and there must be a balance between them." This might sound paradoxical to the purist, but the realities on the ground being what they were the Nepali Congress had scarcely any alternative to this approach.

Whatever else it might or might not have achieved, the revolution forced the kingdom to drop its veil. From the half-light of feudalism Nepal was suddenly exposed to the blazing light of democracy. The country was not prepared for such a sudden encounter. Though it had technically remained free all along, it was one of Asia's most backward countries, socially, politically and economically. Nepalese society was in no shape, not even remotely, to work democratic institutions. Indeed, when the country was called upon to experiment with the most sophisticated and rational system of polity that man has yet been able to devise it just did not know which way to turn.

How difficult the situation was may well be imagined if it is remembered that such expressions as vote, election, people's representative and parliament were totally unknown to the idiom of the land. The bewilderment of the Nepalese only increased when they were told that every man was his own master, that it was their inherent right to determine how the country should be governed and by whom. There was the challenge of integrating 10 million people of diverse races, religions, languages and cultures into one nation. They were, legally spcaking, the emphasis being on the word "legally." By legalistic definition Nepal was a nation. It had the three major attributes of nationhood—torritory, a central political authority to which all the citizens owed allegiance, and sovereignty. Still, as a random collection of musical instruments cannot produce a symphony, the voice of the Nepalese nation could not conceal a recurring strain of dissonance and disharmony. Nepalese society did not think, much less act, in a manner that any integrated society elsewhere did. There was an absence of a feeling of oneness, of a sense of belonging, of total commitment. This was much too real to be wished away.

The mental horizon of Nepal society did not extend to encompass the nation as a whole. It narrowed only to accommodate a given group or community. In other words, not every Nepalese felt he was as much an integral part of the nation as any other Nepalese, that the nation would be poorer to the extent that he would disengage himself from the mainstream of life. That was not particularly a Nepalese problem. Most transitional societies suffered more or less from this malaise. But, for reasons rooted in history, the nature of the problem had a complex dimension added to it in Nepal that was not evident in most other areas of the third world. Innumerable contradictory strands had been introduced into the national matrix.

The problem, then, was to transform Nepalese society, with its limited horizontal mobility, into a society with unlimited vertical mobility. There were two diametrically opposite paths to the solution of the problem: the classic path of coercion, that is application of force at all levels, social, political and economic: and the path of consent and persuasion. The Nepali Congress opted for the second path in order to reconstruct the national society. But there was more to it than just that. Implicit in it was the task of nation-building and the establishment of a clear Nepalese identity to which the men who had made the revolution pledged themselves.

The magnitude of the undertaking could be appreciated if it is remembered that "nation-building itself involves more than just the establishment of the most complex of modern organisations, the machinery of state; it also entails the creation of a host of organisations within the society. In the political sphere these would range from organisations capable of articulating the various interests of society to these capable of aggregating these interests in the form of public policies which can become in turn directives for guiding the organisation of the state. In the economic sphere, modernisation involves the formation of a multitude of other type of organisations: firms and factories, systems of communication and transportation and above all, the sensitive market. Socially, modernisation entails the development of an array of organisations that can provide the individual with the necessary range of choice for assooiation, so that whenever he steps beyond the family he can find opportunities to test his talents and to find his full identity as a social and a psychological being." If the revolution hastened the process of breaking up the structure of the traditional society, it also posed the problem of eonstructing a modern society· This was the complex and demanding problem the Nepali Congress faced.

But the party was obliged to accept the "middle way" to change instead of going in for the total liquidation of the Rana regime, which might have left it relatively unfettered to pursue its objeetive. Though shaken, the power base of the Ranas had not crumbled. The Congress understandably had a hard row to hoe when it entered into partnership with Mohan Shumsher in February 1951 to work the coalition government. The situation could be summed up thus:

(*a*) King Tribhuvan emerged as the key factor internally.

(*b*) Mohan Shumsher, though ruffied, still calculated in terms of retrieving as much of his lost powers and privileges as possible.

(*c*) The Nepali Congress was in a considerably disillusioned mood, with swelling ranks of critics within the party and outside.

(*d*) India found itself in a rather comfortable position from where it could pull strings so that Nepal might not disagree to adapt its policy to the broad framework of India's northern frontier policy in particular and foreign policy in general.

Amid cheers of welcome from a vast multitude of people, not excluding Mohan Shumsher, King Tribhuvan returned to Kathmandu on 15 February 1951. The Rana patriarch's presence at Gauchar airfield to receive the ruler whom he had forced to flee his kingdom only some months earlier sharply focused the changes that had meanwhile taken place in Nepal. The tone, temper and orientation of the new political order was set by the proclamation the King issued on 18 February 1951. A ten-member coalition government, consisting of five representatives each of the Nepali Congress and the Rana group was formed with Mohan Shumsher and B.P. Koirala as Prime Minister and Home Minister respectively.

The experiment commenced only to fail. Though the Ranas had lost much of their power, they made every attempt to salvage as much of it as they could. Koirala on the other hand made no particular effort not to put his cards on the table. His words and deeds made it clear that he had not joined the government only to earn his right to a pension. The party had given him a mandate, and he would do whatever was necessary to execute it. While King Tribhuvan, the most important factor in the equation, succinctly emphasised the fact that he constituted the one indivisible source of power in the state.

From the very outset the King made it plain that there was no love lost between him and his Prime Minister. He did not say this in so many words, but that was what he meant. His emphasis seemed to mean two points: King Tribhuvan had no desire to be anybody's tool, and Mohan Shumsher would be suffered not a day longer than absolutely necessary. Much earlier than many had anticipated, the King indicated that he would like to be unburdened of his Prime Minister. And he sought to persuade the Home Minister to support this move. In the words of B.P. Koirala, the King "wanted to get rid of Mohan Shumsher and he wanted me to assist him in this regard."

But Koirala would not lend himself to the scheme. He had his own reasons for not doing so. For one thing, he "found Mohan Shumsher was not hindering me. He was some kind of a scapegoat. Whenever there would be trouble, the blame could be laid on him." For another, Koirala did not summarily dismiss Mohan Shumsher's warning that "ultimately my trouble would be with the King . . . According to him [Mohan Shumsher] the power that would be taken away from him would not be handed over to the people. This would go to the King . . . he suggested that it would be in our interest to have him as Prime Minister, because in that case we would have greater manoeuvrability."

That the logic of the argument was not lost upon Koirala was borne out by his observation that he "was not particularly inclined to take action against Mohan Shumsher." And that because, every other reason besides. Koirala "did not want the King to step into the Rama's shoes . . . I felt that we should make him from the very shart a constitutional head. He should not be permitted to interfere with the day-to-day administration of the country." Not that he wanted to do away with the institution of monarchy. Far from it. Much to the ire of some of his colleagues, he was "dead opposed to the idea of the abolition of the institution of monarchy. Because I thought the monarch was the symbol of national unity and the symbol of continuity of the state . . . I did not do anything to harm him or the high status that he had."

For our purpose it is not necessary to give a very detailed account of the political developments between 1951, when the Rana-Nepali Congress coalition government was formed, and 1959, when the country got its first truly representative government. Suffice it to say that in the years between the termination of the struggle and King Mahendra's assumption of power the democratic process was worked as if to prove that it was unworkable. The parties to the democratic game, with the exception of Koirala and some of his close associates such as Ganesh Man Singh and Subarna Shumsher, vied with each other to establish that there was no substitute for democracy but that the wrong set of men had been entrusted with the task of operating it.

Apart from the Rana group every-other opposition party—a sizable number of opposition political outfits had in the meantime mushroomed—made sustained efforts to throw a spanner into the works. The main force of the opposition attack was however directed against the Nepali Congress, particularly B.P. Koirala. Of the opposition parties the newly rigged-up Gurkha Dal, a past-regarding Rana outfit, was relatively powerful. The fact that the party's general secretary was Bharat Shumsher, a grandson of Babar Shumsher, Defence Minister in the Rana-Congress coalition Cabinet and brother of Mohan Shumsher, whould give a sufficiently broad hint about its political orientation. Among the oher opposition parties mention may be made of D.R. Regmi's Napali Rashtriya Congress, Tanka Prasad Acharya's Praja Parishad and the Communist Party.

As for King Tribhuvan, he was not quite cut out for the role history and circumstances had forced on him. It is said that he even toyed at one stage with the idea of getting Nepal a place within the framework of the Indian polity. Be that as it may, he had established a certain understanding with the Nepali Congress and was not averse to giving B.P. Koirala an edge over the others. But that was about all. The King had no intention of permitting any politician to emerge as a balancing factor. Also, the emerging pattern of development only strengthened his opinion that the Rana group would have to be kept in its place. But it was another matter so far as Mohan Shumsher was concerned. There were indications, and that too quite early, that the King was in no mood to put up with Mohan Shumsher as his Prime Minister. This was one of the important issues in the initial stages which found the King and Koirala on opposite sides of the spectrum.

Koirala's major problem was neither the opposition parties nor his not very encouraging relations with the King. Although the main thrust of the opposition parties was directed against the Nepali Congress and not the other partner, the Rana group, in the coalition government, this did not worry him overmuch. He was well aware that the opposition parties were neither individually or unitedly in any shape to offer him serious opposition. As regards King Tribhuvan things had not, at least yet, reaehed the point of no return. The differences between the King and Koirala at this stage were more on the question of modalities and less on any basic issue. And Koirala could easily ignore the opposition parties with their almost national existence and dependence on totally unprincipled politics.

But he could ill afford to ignore the growing volume and extent of interparty conflict. It was no secret that M.P. Koirala, President of the Nepali Congress, heartily disagreed with the Home Minister on almost every major issue. The area of disagreement between the formal steward of the party and its chief spokesman in the ruling coalition was too extensive not to affect the political situation adversely. That the party president's exclusion from the coalition government also had its impact on the whole setup would be hard to contradict. To the consternation of B.P. Koirala and his colleagues a campaign soon started to the effect that the party representatives in the Cabinet were not serious about removing the Rana group from power. It was evidently inspired by M.P. Koirala and his friends. It was also bandied about that unless Mohan Shumsher and his men were obliged to bow out of the geo-politically, it was very much in India's interest to redeem its pledges to the people. A conflict situation developed so fast that even the usually alert B.P. Koirala could not control it in time.

A scrutiny of India's policy towards the kingdom would be in order at this point. Ideologically, economically and geo-politically, it was very much in India's interest to ensure that the democratic experiment in Nepal did not founder. The fast-changing political scenario up north after China's annexation of Tibet did not fail to convey its import to the formulators of India's policy towards the Himalayan region. Nehru could not be accused of not naving viewed these developments in a wider historical perspective. The "middle-way" approach had not yet been abandoned, it is true. Still whenever an opportunity came his way, he made it clear that one of the three factors—the Rana group, to be precise—in the Nepalese equation would have to be eliminated sooner than later.

Subsequent developments in Nepal substantiated this view. Thinking on the institution of monarchy was that it had not outlived its utility, and must therefore have a reasonable place within the total framework of the Napalese polity. New Delhi agreed with B.P. Koirala's assessment that the monarchy, much as it constituted an integrating agency in the given context, must be persuaded to reign and not rule. That is, the country must make every effort to get the parties concerned to accept the concept of constitutional, and not absolute, monarchy.

Underlying all this was the fact that India's "interest in the internal conditions of Nepal", as Nehru candidly admitted, "has become still more acute and personal in view of the developments across our borders in China and Tibet." Nehru did not leave it at that. For the benefit of those who might still doubt the basic considerations which influenced India's policy towards Nepal, he stated that, besides "our sympathetic interest in Nepal, we are also interested in the security of our own country. . . Much as we stand for the independence of Nepal, we cannot allow anything to go wrong in Nepal or permit that barrier [the Himalayas] to be crossed or wrecked, because that would be a risk to our own security."

The Indian government candidly admitted that altruism was not the motivating factor of its Nepal policy. If it saw fit to accommodate itself to the changed circumstances it also was firmly of the opinion that no extraneous consideration should override India's security requirements. This aspect of Indian policy was not a secret. But to spell out this policy was one thing, to implement it another. There was a great deal of difference between what New Delhi desired and what its man on the scene did.

India's ambassador in Kathmandu at that time was C.P.N. Singh, a member of the landed aristocracy. Singh earned a knighthood for his faithful service to the British, particularly as a leader of the so-called national war front (which all genuine nationalists heartily despised) in the second world war. He was ill fitted for such a complex and demanding assignment. He tended to take the Nepalese, from the Prime Minister down, for granted, and his imperious manner often complicated matters for both the Nepali Congress and India. Others apart, Home

Minister Koirala bitterly complained that "the Indian Ambassador never visited the Secretariat. Whenever he had to meet a minister, he would send for him."

A plausible explanation of the fact that Singh got away with his style of diplomacy could be that the conduct of India's foreign affairs at that time lacked the necessary systematisation. It is rightly said that "India inherited a full-fledged secretariat structure for internal administration from the British but had to create an External Affairs Ministry after 1947. Some of the early Indian ambassadors, such as Sardar K.M. Panikkar in China and C.P.N. Singh in Nepal, were allowed considerable latitude in the implementation of foreign policy because of the inadequate institutionalisation of their roles." It needs to be added that this "latitude" did not prove counter-productive in certain cases.

In theory India's policy towards Nepal had little to take exception to. Between the two countries, that is between the ruling Indian National Congress and the Nepali Congress, there was a certain identity of views so far as the emerging pattern of politics in the north was concerned. Not only India's ruling party but also most of the opposition parties firmly believed that Nepal was a basic factor in India's security. The views of the Nepali Congress on matters concerning the security of Nepal's northern frontier did not at that point run counter to India's stance on the defence of the Himalayan region. The other aspect of India-Nepal relations was the kingdom's experiment with democracy. The two countries shared broadly one another's views also on this issue.

Still, not long after the Rana-Nepali Congress partnership had got off to a not quite flying start, things seemed to go wrong. Despite New Delhi's seemingly best efforts not to put its wrong foot forward the image it projected in Kathmandu was not exactly what it wanted. An active and fairly extensive anti-Indian lobby emerged in Kathmandu through a combination of factors, among them over-eagerness to be helpful, a growing tendency to strike a self-righteous posture and, above all, the unimaginative and assertive functioning of the Indian

Embassy. For whatever went wrong, and much did go wrong in those days, India was held responsible.

Motives were imputed to almost every step New Delhi took to ensure that the embryonic democratic experiment got a fair chance of survival. The diverse and often mutually quarrelling political parties and groups used India as whipping-boy, each for its own calculations, when it suited their purpose. Even the Nepali Congress was no exception, if not for any other reason at least to escape the opprobrium of being an echo of New Delhi. For instence, the party's Working Committee adopted in March 1953 a resolution to the effect that "in the interest of a healthy relationship between India and Nepal and with a view to thwarting attempts at fostering misunderstanding between the peoples of the two countries, we feel that the remaining part of the army reorganisation and training programme can be handled by our officers and men, and we resolve that the Nepali government should now request the Government of India to withdraw its military mission."

Mention might also be made of the statement B.P. Koirala made after the turbulent demonstration which greeted the arrival of an Indian parliamentary goodwill mission in Kathmandu: "I agree that the incident was unfortunate, but we must not be jittery about it . . . and refuse to see reality. The Kosi agreement, the presence of an Indian military mission, a large contingent of Indian advisers and technicians, and the India-Nepal trade agreement have been irritating the national sentiments of the Nepalese people. . . . The incident at the airport was not an organised event but an outburst of pentup feeling."

This attempt to explain away the situation implied that the anti-Indian syndrome in Kathmandu was too real to be ignored and that the Nepali Congress intended to exploit it if necessary. A fallout of anti-Indian sentiment was that it came to serve as a foil after a sort to the country's unfolding sense of nationalism. It is not wide of the mark to say that "because the kingdom had never been colonised there had previously been no focus for nationalism. Now India, resented by those who foresaw the failure of their hopes for the country—and in the case of politicians who did not get into office for themselves—provided the required focus."

The Nepali Congress leadership, as represented by B.P. Koirala, Subarna Shumsher and Ganesh Man Singh, did not have much ground for believing that the disorganised and divergent opposition groups could damage the party if its sense of historical realism was not warped. Internal dissension, resulting as much from ideological incompatibility as from the struggle for power, split the party ranks. The party president, M.P. Koirala, had not been included in the first coalition Cabinet, and he neither forgot nor forgave this slight. It was insinuated that B.P. Koirala and some other Nepali Congress ministers did not mean to carry out the party's objective of dislodging the Ranas from power, thus jeopardising the prospect of a full-fledged Congress government. The dissidents explained this was why Mohan Shumsher continued throwing a spanner in the works. The failure of the Congress leaders to implement expeditiously its political and economic programme added grist to the opposition mill. To forestall this they argued it was necessary for B.P. Koirala to make room for a more dynamic personality, and his opponents in the party soon fastened themselves to M.P. Koirala.

At another level, such mutually exclusive political elements as the Gurkha Dal, K.I. Singh (a Nepali Congress leader who opposed the 1951 Delhi agreement) and his men, D.R. Regmi's Nepali Rashtriya Congress, and the Communist Party worked overtime to keep up the pressure on the segment of the Nepali Congress which owned allegiance to B.P. Koirala. What added fuel to the fire was his repeated emphasis on the concept of constitutional monarchy and the assertion that "the motive force of the recent revolution in Nepal was the demand for a just solution of land problems whereby feudal exploitation of the peasantry would end." The King became perturbed, even though he wanted the democratic experiment to survive, lest B.P. Koirala do something that might again fetter the monarchy. And the feudal elements, still the country's most organised pressure group, got panicky.

The resultant situation saw the King and B.P. Koirala, the two men who should have come very much closer to each other in the country's interests, walking rapidly in opposite directions. Their relations became strained, much to Koirala's disadvantage. M.P. Koirala threw himself into the breach. But B.P. Koirala appeared determined to stick to the party's pledges to the people even at the risk of closing all his options. By and large, he had the party's rank and file with him. He also enjoyed the unqualified support of Ganesh Man Singh, the second most powerful man in the party. The advantages were however far outweighed by the disadvantages. For Home Minister Koirala "took on more than I could manage. I took on the King. I said no power to the King. I took on India and said no interference from India. And then I took on the Ranas and the feudal landlords. There was a difference of opinion between M.P. Koirala—he was president of the party—and myself over all these issues.

"He had a very strong point of view. . . . We differed on three questions. He said: 'Because of the revolution theree is already a law and order problem. On top of this if you introduce land reforms, you will turn the situation worse. . . .' My argument was that law and order would be restored only when we went along with our commitment to the people regarding land reforms . . . This was therefore the time when we should introduce drastic land reforms . . . Another point on which we disagreed was the role of the Ranas and the King. I said the King must function as a constitutional monarch. Once you give him the role to act arbitrarily, then another revolution will be necessary for saving democracy. Then he said: 'No. You are functioning by virtue of authority vested in you by the King, you have derived the constitutional right from him. He is the constitution, he is the lawgiver and you are there as his nominee.' I said: 'This is too legalistic a point of view. I am here because of the revolution, my legitimacy does not depend on the King.' Vaguely the difference was also on the role of India. I said that India must not permit a situation to be created where we are dubbed anti-national brokers of India, as the Ranas were saying."

The Westminster variety of parliamentary democracy had to be worked in a country that was just not prepared for it. The kingdom was without a common focus except the monarchy, and it totally lacked the political and economic premises for democracy. In this sharply uneven struggle it was imperative that B.P. Koirala should have allies. Who could be his allies other than the party, the people and the King, in that order? But the party was ideologically confused and strife-torn, the people were apathetic, and the King was in a sullen mood. Events overtook the Home Minister. In spite of his intention not to cross swords with Mohan Shumsher merely for effect, the inherent contradictions of the Rana-Nepali Congress coalition compelled him before long to precipitate matters. The situation took a menacing turn when the Gurkha Dal rebelled in the Kathmandu Valley and K.I. Singh resorted to terrorism. Unable to cope with his group's widespread terrorist activities in the western region adjoining the India-Nepal border, Kathmandu sought New Delhi's assistance not only to get over the immediate problem but also to train the Nepalese Army. And the appearance in Kathmandu of an Indian military mission in 1952 provided a tangible object on which to focus the not as yet strong anti-Indian feeling.

It might well be said that the disturbances the Gurkha Dal engineered in April 1951 were the starting point of the process of elimination of the country's alternative power centre—the monarchy. The Dal militant not only raided the residence of Home Minister Koirala, compelling him thereby to order the shooting of one of them. They also demonstrated in front of the royal palace, demanding restoration of the Rana regime. This alarmed King Tribhuvan. He relieved Prime Minister Mohan Shumsher of control of the army and took over himself the office of Commander-in-Chief that had been the Rana family's exclusive preserve for over a century. Other changes in the army establishment, the King's public condemnation of the Gurkha Dal agitation, and his upholding the Home Minister's action resulting in the death of a raider—all this indicated that the Palace did not intend to have its writ restricted to its compound.

King Tribhuvan was now determined to get rid of his Prime Minister. Shrewd as he was, Mohan Shumsher could not be said to be unaware of this. This partly explains his subsequent attempts to curry favour with the Nepali Congress. It was not without a purpose that the Rana group made it possible for the coalition Cabinet to accept unanimously the principle that *birta* land should be abolished, notwithstanding that they stood to lose most thereby. But that did not prevent events from taking their course. As promised earlier, the King announced on 2 October the constitution of a 35 member advisory assembly, consisting mostly of Nepali Congress activists and some non-party men. Mohan Shumsher was kept in the dark about this move, and his group was not allowed any representation in the proposed assembly. He openly expressed his resentment, and this was his swansong.

Another 40 days and the curtain fell on the man who symbolised all that the revolution had been waged against. The irony of circumstances was however that the incident which ultimately forced him into oblivion also obliged the man who made the revolution to quit the scene. This incident deserves to be recapitulated in some detail. In view of the deterioration in law and order the Home Minister had decreed that no public meeting should be held in the valley without obtaining at least a prior sanction of 24 hours from the police. The opposition groups resented the order, and their chief target of attack was the Home Minister. Encouraged by them, a group of students held a meeting on 6 November in violation of the order and the police arrested some of their leaders. A crowd collected at the police station and demanded the release of the arrested persons. One thing led to another and the police opened fire without the Home Minister's authorisation, resulting in the death of one student and injury to two others.

How did Koirala explain his conduct? He said: "I learnt of that incident about half an hour after it had occurred. There was a prohibitory order against public demonstrations, against holding meetings. In the morning the students had come to me and told me that they were going to violate that prohibitory order by holding a meeting. I told them that they could inform the police and hold the meeting . . . I told them that, for students, it was enough if they informed the police that they would be holding a public meeting. Or if they did not want to do that, they could tell me formally that they would be holding a meeting. There was no difficulty about that. They said no, they were going to break the law . . . the prohibitory order. I said that in that case they would have to bear the consequences. But I instructed the police to the effect that they should not interfere because I wanted the students to give vent to their pentup feeling. The prohibitory order was specifically meant for the political parties and not for the students. I told the police authorities that they should not interfere with the students' programme. In the afternoon they held a meeting at Tundikhel. There was no disturbance and the police did not do anything. They went to the police station, where they tried to snatch a rifle from a police guard, and then the police opened fire. But, I did not know that there had been police firing till a PTI (Press Trust of India) man or some other Indian journalist who had been covering the incident came running to me to inquire whether I knew of the firing. I said that I did not know. I categorically told him that there was no firing. Then he said that he had seen the firing. As a matter of fact, he saw some of the boys being hit. I telephoned the police headquarters and they confirmed that there had been a firing. So there was no question of my ordering the police firing on the students."

The valley echoed as Prime Minister Mohan Shumsher condemned the police firing in good, round terms. Evidently, he made an attempt to make a public issue of the police firing, which Koirala took as a personal attack on himself. In the course of a press interview on 10 November, Koirala made no bones about the fact that there would be "no peace or democracy in Nepal until the present Prime Minister, Maharaja Mohan Shumsher, goes out of the Cabinet. We have told King Tribhuvan that the Prime Minister's exist is imperative. I have a strong suspicion that reactionary forces are trying to stage an autocratic comeback by creating chaos and taking advantage of the recurrent emotional disturbances."

The Home Minister's press statement did not contain anything that might conflict with the King's scheme of things. What however grated on the King was Koirala's broadcast to the people. Having owned responsibility for the police firing, Koirala observed, in a broadcast on 10 November, that the party had compromised with the Ranas in the hope that this might ensure a less-tormented period of transition. But that hope had been "dashed to the ground." He also urged the people to be prepared for a larger struggle to realise the as yet unfulfilled objectives of the revolution. The King understandably had no reason to appreciate this, much less so Koirala's refusal to appear in sackcloth and ashes and mollify the agitating students, who were determined to continue their fight against the "dictatorship of the Rana-Koirala axis." That was enough to confirm the King's growing doubts about the malleability of the Home Minister.

In the circumstances, both the Prime Minister and the Home Minister followed the only course open to them. They resigned. On 16 November, King Tribhuvan appointed M.P. Koirala Prime Minister, ignoring the intense resentment and not a little opposition this engendered in the ranks of the Nepali Congress. Thus the president of the Nepali Congress became the Himalayan kingdom's first commoner to hold the office of Prime Minister, albeit on the sufferance of the Palace. The process of concentration of power in the Crown that had started with the Delhi agreement also came full circle. As to why he was unacceptable to the King as first Minister. B.P. Koirala observed: "In the beginning King Tribhuvan and myself pulled on very well . . . But on the question of power the King did not want to relent. In fact, he wanted to get more power for himself, for the Crown, for the King, Whereas I wanted that the King should start functioning as a constitutional monarch right from the outset . . . He (the King) thought that if I was made Prime Minister the King would be just a constitutional head. India also perhaps did not like my being Prime Minister. On the question of India also, M.P. Koirala was more amenable, more soft I should say. These were the two important considerations why the King did not choose me as a Prime Minister.

A State of Flux

Prime Minister M.P. Koirala, who had by now developed considerable difference of opinion with B.P. Koirala, formed a composite government of sorts which included eight Nepali Congressmen and six non-party men with as many divergent political views. From the very outset the new Prime Minister had to face heavy weather, what with his deepening conflict with the party, particularly B.P. Koirala, and his timid approach to the crisis in the country. This did not allow any significant advance to be made in respect of badly needed reforms, social, political or economic. He refused to abide by the party Working Committee's decision requiring him to reconstitute the Cabinet on the basis of a list of seven it had prepared. The upshot was that the rift beween the Prime Minister and the party widened. Eventually, M.P. Koirala and two other ministers, Mahabir Shumsher and Mahendra Bikram Shah, were expelled from the party on 25 July 1952.

A meeting of the Prime Minister's followers in Kathmandu on 26 July condemned the expulsion most vehemently, accusing the Nepali Congress Working Committee of usurping power through "conspiracy, intrigue and party clique." This prompted Tanka Prasad Acharya and D.R. Regmi, whose opposition to the Nepali Congress was total and who had meanwhile rigged up the National Democratic United Front, which included the Communist Party and some Nepali Congress dissidents, to observe that the Congress "was torn by factional and family fights and had ceased to represent anyone except a coterie." To fight his case at the ensuing session of the Mahasamiti, or Nepali Congress Committee, as a "common soldier of the Congress and not as Prime Minister," M.P. Koirala resigned from the prime ministership on 10 August. But that was of no avail, for only six out of the Mahasamiti's 108 members supported him. Some months later, in May 1953, he formed a new party, the National Democratic Party, with himself and Mahendra Bikram Shah as president and secretary respectively.

Between M.P. Koirala's exit from office in August 1952 and is hreappointment as Prime Minister in June 1953 the King personally assumed power. On 14 August 1952, he announced the appointment of a six-man committee of Royal Councillors to assist him in the business of government, particularly "eradication of bribery, corruption, and nepotism in the government, establishment of an independent judiciary, and an unambiguous definition of the people's fundamental rights. The line of action King Tribhuvan opted for would clearly indicate that, besides other things, he would not entrust the Nepal Congress, apparently the largest national party, with power. Of course it did not follow that the King had despaired of the country's experiment with democracy. None other than B.P. Koirala confirmed that King Tribhuvan used to give all authority to the one he appointed Prime Minister. He did not want to rule directly although he did not want to give up any constitutional rights. But in the exercise of those rights he used to trust others who commanded his confidence. He had democratic inclinations.

The Councillors' regime did not last longer than ten months. On 15 June 1953, M.P. Koirala, leader of the 45-day-old National Democratic Party, was once again summoned to form a government. His performance this time was as indifferent as it had been on the last occasion. Totally devoid of any popular support and lacking a sense of direction and purpose, the government temporised when it ought to have acted. Hardly eight months passed when the King had the National Democratic Party government replaced by a four-party "national coatition" comprising the National Democratic Party, the Nepali Rashtriya Congress, the Praja Parishad, and the All-Nepal Jana Congress led by Bhadrakali Mishra, a former Nepali Congress activist, with M.P. Koirala as Prime Minister.

This was installed in office on 18 February, the kingdom's National Day. In a no-nonsense message King Tribhuvan reminded the new government that "the atmosphere of political instability and uncertainty that has arisen in the country today can benefit neither the country nor the people. If this uncertainty continues for long, it will prove fatal . . . the existing situation in the country has filled the people with a sense of frustration and apathy." The King still hoped that the parties and politicians would recover their sense of perspective, that they would stop the rot before it was too late.

His admonition fell on deaf ears. Unable to face the realities of the situation, the government employed all, its energies merely to keep itself afloat. In the process it got sucked deeper into the quagmire of confusion and mindless pursuit of power. The economy stagnated; unemployment increased sickeningly; the administrative machinery was at the nadir of its efficiency; and the tentacles of corruption held society in a vicelike grip. The coalition partners, at feud with one another from the very beginning, created the impression that they were committed to a policy of scuttle, Prime Minister M.P. Koirala surely did not contradict this when he said in the course of a press interview, on 12 December 1954, that "the purpose for which the present government was formed has been completely defeated."

To cap it all, the opposition parties, mainly the Nepali Congress, went at the coalition hammer and tongs. They accused it of every conceivable kind of misconduct. As if to lend credence to this, Tanka Prasad Acharya and Bhadrakali Mishra, who had been forced to quit the Cabinet, said: "The independence of the judiciary is lost. All over the country anarchy, famine, corruption, bribery, unemployment and inflation are rampant. . . . The peasants are exploited more than ever. Facilities for communication, irrigation, education and public health are almost non-existent. The lawful rights of students, labour, women and merchants have been ruthlessly suppressed Reactionary elements are receiving full encouragement. . . . Big landlords and capitalists are having a field day in exploiting the people." On 2 March 1955, M.P. Koirala's second term of office formally ended as dismally as his first. Since failing health had obliged King Tribhuvan to go abroad for medical treatment, it was Crown Prince Mahendra who, duly authorised to act on behalf of the King, accepted the resignation of the government.

At this point we might pause to observe the pattern of relations between the political parties and the Palace. Some of these parties, not excluding the Nepali Congress, seemed to have made it a point to focus their critical attention on the Palace almost from the outset. They accused the Palace of various acts of omission and commission, ranging from power lust to graft. The critics of the Palace had a method in all they did. They made a careful distinction between King Tribhuvan and Crown Prince Mahendra. So far as the King was concerned, criticism was in a low key. Almost always the critics avoided being personal. Not so with the Crown Prince. Deliberately or otherwise, he was made the target of criticism that was often personal, and a severe hurt to his pride to boot. All the gossip, rumours and whispers of scandal that went round the valley could not possibly have any objective besides driving a wedge between the King and the heir-apparent and throwing a lurid light on the Crown Prince.

Every day that passed seemed to add to the list of misdemeanours the Prince was allegedly guilty of. One day it would be said that King Tribhuvan wanted to disinherit him because he was impatient to succeed his father and hence had engineered a conspiracy against him. At another hints would be dropped that he was given to draft, corruption and what have you. Mahendra chose not to take this campaign lying down. Five months had barely passed since when he decided to take the field. In a statement on 28 July the formation of the Rana-Congress coalition government 1951 he said: "Nepal, our motherland, was groaning under the boots of autocratic rulers for quite a long time. In a situation like this people could not attain happiness or prosperity . . . it was imperative that something had to be done to elevate the political, social and economic standard of the people. . . . In this 20th century it has become an irrefutable fact that unless the governance of a country is placed on sound democratic lines the country and its people cannot hope to prosper. . . . In Nepal, a democratic system of government was brought into being. Democracy in its true sense could be possible only when people would doff their sectional interests, when they would stop going about shouting slogans and vitiating the political climate; when they would awaken their latent national feelings and divert their energies to nation-building activities. But I have found that some people have identified democracy with licence, to make disturbances and go about spreading wild rumours. In some quarters, I am aware, rumours are being spread that my august father and myself are at cros-spurposes . . . that I am aligning myself with the Gurkha Dal. To hear such rumours saddens me, and sometimes even nauseates me."

This indicates that the Crown Prince has been forming quite at an early stage in the country's democratic experiment his opinion of the parties and politicians. He maintained a keen vigil lest he should be caught on the wrong foot. On 18 September 1951, he issued a statement saying that "my attention has been invited . . . to a wild rumour being screeched by the Nepali Rashtriya Congress (D.R. Regmi's party) to the effect that His Royal Highness the Crown Prince is partieipating in the anti-government demonstration being staged by it. . . I would categorically say that this is a malicious lie. . . . In Nepal today, parties are having a mushroom growth. It has become a commonplace here for one party to be organised this day and be split up the very next. From the third day such parties would forget all about their aims and objectives and would be busy flinging mud at one another."

Only a few months had elapsed after the political changes in the country. Yet Mahendra found enough justification to condemn the political parties and their method of operation. The campaign against him went on unabated, obliging him thereby to defend himself publicly. In a surprisingly rancorous message to the nation on 18 February 1952, the first National Democracy Day, he said: "It is under the leadership, and only under the leadership, of our King that the people and the country can hope to thrive and prosper. Let us not hearken to the lies screeched by the rumourmongers; let us be loyal to the King . . . untold number of political factions have come up . . . factions led by a handful of selfish opportunists . . . corruption is rife. . . . Freedom of speech is there, but grievances go unheard. . . . Rules and regulations are being raped in the name of democracy. . . . For all this, can we ever hold our King responsible? I would not do so even if injustice has been done to me. . . . To tell the truth, it was the saboteurs and the anti-nationals who have tarnished the fair name of liberty by their perfidies. . . . I have this to say, that our one-year-old democracy is willy nilly lying on its deathbed."

The balance-sheet of the 12-month-old democractic experiment, as drawn up by the Crown Prince, made gloomy reading. He considered the political parties the roof of all evil and he directed his attack at them. The brief for King Tribhuvan was essentially a defence of the institution of monarchy. Once again Mahendra felt constrained to say that his "attention has been drawn to the propagation of fabricated propaganda in respect of my relations with my august father both by self-motivated groups and individuals. Such propaganda does not have any basis or reality." But for him there was no respite from this campaign. The growing criticism, at times scurrilous, of the monarchy was something that almost every political party indulged in. They had their reasons. To the extent that their inability to act and to determine the course of politics increased, the monarchy gained. The parties resented this intensely, but there was little they could do about it. And their attempt to hold the Palace responsible for whatever went wrong in the country angered the Crown Prince much more than the King himself. It also aroused his suspicion that the parties wanted to pull down the institution of monarchy itself.

This was reflected in a statement he issued on 31 August 1953: "I hear that the cinema hall being opened recently in Pakanajol is rumoured to belong to me. But should anybody sloop to convert our true democracy and democratic freedoms through their own corrupt practices into corruptocracy or alienocracy, should anybody in the shelter of a party platform forget the Nepalihood among the Nepali people and shart vilifying one another, I would not make any comment at all. The thing of which everybody has already has more than they can stomach can never play any vital role. As the saying goes, the dogs may . . . bark, the caravan marches on."

As one effete government succeeded another, as the kingdom's problems multiplied in almost geometrical progression, and as the King's failing health stood between him and the business of state, Crown Prince Mahendra came to occupy an increasingly pivotal position in the life of the nation. Over the years from February 1951 he had closely watched the working of the democratic system. He also made some efforts to adjust himself to the changing relations among the political forces in the country. But it appeared to him that there was between him and the ongoing democratic experiment an absolutely irreconcilable point—the role of the monarchy. The emphasis at the people's level of politics, as reflected by the Nepali Congress, was on the fact that the monarchy should be bridled to the extent that it became no more than a figurehead, a decoration merely to be tolerated.

On the other hand, the functioning of the party system made it gradually clear that the monarchy provided the only basis of stability in the country. The democratic system was being operated as if with the sole intention of enabling the monarchy to emerge as the country's only source of effective power. Not unoften it seemed that the politicians, except B.P. Koirala and a couple of his most trusted colleagues, vied with each other in aiding the monarchy to become the one constant factor in Nepalese politics. In this they did not have to go it alone. Others elsewhere also contributed their mite to strengthening the throne. They had various motives, one of the most dominant of which was the desire not to be confronted with a situation that might jeopardise the growth of a multipolarised power structure.

The Crown Prince's view of the Nepalese situation was straight, clear and nearly unidimensional. He had no romantic notions that the kingdom had a message to deliver or a messianic part to play on the world stage. There was nothing to suggest that he was not aware that his was a poor, backward and illiterate country which depended not a little on foreign aid and the earnings of its citizens as mercenaries in foreign armies. But he was a proud man and Nepal was his obsession. Mahendra was also an embittered man, thanks not a little to his not very happy relationship with his father and the spiteful campaign the political parties were systematically conducting against him.

In the course of his Vijaya Dashami (the day of triumph over injustice and darkness) message on ? October 1954, Crown Prince Mahendra observed: "The mud and slime of the rains have dried up, the clouds and gloom have been swept away from the skies; the autumnal blue is overhead; and the greenery of the earth and the waves over the golden ricefields give us new hopes and new aspirations . . . There is some restlessness, some suffocation in the country. The failure of the political revolution to deliver the goods is casting its shadow on us. That is by no means a happy augury . . . Instead of shouting empty slogans regarding foreign intervention we should all be united and forge ahead. Only then will others not make capital out of our weaknesses. The question of foreign intervention or non-intervention is also a question of our responsibility . . . From our friendly countries we have been receiving not only assurances but tangible assistance in resources for the development of our country. It is we who should make good use of this assistance and co-operation."

The message was delivered at a time the political scene looked disconcertingly twisted. A number of experiments to give the country a reasonably stable and work-oriented government had gone bad. Political bickerings were increasing, and the party system seemed to be disintegrating. There was widespread anti-Indian agitation in the country and M.P. Koirala's "national coalition" government, which as a matter of policy excluded the Nepali Congress, the country's largest political party; was impotently in office although King Tribhuvan had entrusted the Prime Minister with sweeping power.

The Crown Prince, as the representative of the King, took a dim view of this state of affairs. If he was not particularly enamoured of M.P. Koirala's lame-duck show, he had not yet changed his opinion on India's role in Nepal. That would explain his pointed reference to those who had raised the bogey of external interference, which at that point obviously meant India, with the kingdom's domestic affairs. The message also revealed that he had made his own assessment of the working of the Nepalese polity since the 1950-51 struggle. The categorical reference to the "failure of the political revolution" was not meant just for effect. To him this concerned what he emphasised was a fact of life, and he emphasised it not without a purpose. He was building up a case against the party system. He was also establishing a direct dialogue with the people.

So far as that went, he was not inconsistent. He had been at it since the introduction of parliamentary democracy in Nepal. The other points he sought to underline could be thus summed up: the institution of monarchy stood for democracy, nationalism, Nepalihood or Nepali consciousness, a clean society and economic development, while the political parties were the very antithesis of these. As if to drive the message home the Crown Prince, who had already been vested with full "royal authority," observed on 10 February 1955: "It has been almost four years since the inception of democracy in our country. But we have to search and research to find even four achievements to our credit in the meanwhile. It is really a matter of great pity. Should we say that democracy is in a state of infancy, evil propensities like selfishness, greed and envy are very much noticeable in it, which are unnatural for an infant? Should we say that it has already grown up? It is rather unfortunate that symptoms of growth are noticeable nowhere, a fact which is not at all hidden from my countrymen."

A review of the style and operation of the political parties in the period between 18 February 1951, when the Rana-Congress coalition government was formed, and 13 March 1955, when King Tribhuvan died, would show that they failed to comprehend that the social, political and economic conditions in the country militated against the establishment of a viable democracy. They also failed to realise that these conditions could not be changed through the politics of expediency and unprincipled compromise. From the conservative Gurkha Dal to the Communist Party, the political parties and groups did everything best calculated to erode their credibility. Most of what they did, severally or collectively, contributed to stifling the growth of a relatively principled and forward-looking party system. This part could on the one hand strive for a climate reasonably congenial for the people to cultivate a sense of purpose, direction and belonging, and on the other check and balance the country's single power centre, the monarchy.

To a certain extent the Nepali Congress was an exception. Not that it did not at times allow itself to be a victim of its own radical idiom and militant posture. Not infrequently it was confused in its immediate reactions, misread the signs of the time and failed to take its bearings properly. It was not daring enough to opt for the kind of revolutionary politics that might have resolved the deepening crisis. It was also not realist enough to face the fact that "a party is marked by its conditions of birth, its development, the class or alliance of classes that it represents and the social milieu in which it has developed." It was therefore imperative for the party not to miss out on its opportunities to accommodate itself, without compromising the core of its political platform, to the Palace, which was one of the most vital factors in Nepalese politics.

This the Nepali Congress was found wanting in, and the responsibility for it could to a certain degree be traced to B.P. Koirala. An element of overconfidence, impetuosity, arrogance, cynicism and contempt for *realpolitik* marked his attitude toward men and events. In this connexion reference might be made to a letter he wrote the author on 27 November 1952: "I never suffer from frustration; I on the other hand, suffer from overabundance of frivolity. I believe in taking things easy, almost in a jocose mood. Between success and failure the margin is so thin that one slips from one to the other unwittingly and unceasingly."

Nevertheless, it must be admitted that the Nepali Congress, though deliberately kept out of power except for the two brief periods of Rana-Congress coalition and the nominated M.P. Koirala government, did not wither on the vine. Nor did it succumb to the politics of dispersal and disorientation. The leaders of the party, particularly B.P. Koirala, did not plump for the easiest road to power. Whatever his shortcomings, he did not agree to substitute pragmatism—often another name for opportunism—for idealism. If he had agreed to be on the right side of the Palace, the Nepali Congress would not have been denied a place in the power structure. A letter B.P. Koirala wrote the author on 14 October 1954 illustrates this point: "Our King is going to Switzerland. He is already in Calcutta on route. This time again he tried his best to include me in his Cabinet in my individual capacity. I refused because the very basis was wrong and calculated to promote dissension and heterogeneity."

The Nepali Congress turned to its own reconstruction. B.P. Koirala was alive to the fact that ideology was a potent tool that the party must develop from a national platform of sorts into a well-knit organisation with a distinct visage and political philosophy. The search for an ideology brought the party nearer the stream of democratic socialism. It participated in the first and subsequent meets of the Asian Socialist Conference, an organisation of Asian socialist parties, and established close rapport with the Praja Socialist Party of India. Addressing the first Asian Socialist Conference at Rangoon in January 1953, Koirala, as the leader of a four-man Nepalese delegation, observed that the Nepali Congress objectives are democracy and social justice, in other words, socialism and democracy." Along with this the party embarked on a course of agitational politics and nonviolent mass struggle. It petitioned, agitated and struggled for the realisation of the King's promise to convene a constituent assembly elected on the basis of adult suffrage, to frame a democratic constitution and to hold elections. Because of this a sizable number of party activists, not excluding B.P. Koirala and Ganesh Man Singh, suffered incarceration from time to time. In the process the party gained in volume and acquired a seemingly coherent form. It also earned the hostility of powerfully entrenched vested interests, particularly the landowning classes. More, the party alienated the Palace although the party's continuing struggle against feudalism, of which the monarchy had been a prisoner and against which the Congress had staged a revolution, provided a basis of understanding between the two, theoretically at any rate.

Away from his kingdom, with which he seemed to have a love-hate relationship, away from his people, for whom history had ordained that he should become the liberator, away from all the worries, tribulations and conflicts, all the meanness, pettifoggery and small interests, courtiers, sycophants and irresponsible politicians, King Tribhuvan breathed his last in Switzerland. The King is dead, long live the King, the Nepalese exclaimed on 13 March 1955. Nepal had severed its ties with the past. Or so it seemed.

By every account the man who ascended the throne was different from his predecessor. King Mahendra was no ordinary ruler. He had very definite ideas about men and things. Yet he did not seem impervious to the opinions of others, within limits. He had still to make up his mind about the ongoing experiment with democracy. But he was fiercely proud, committed to a rigid personal framework of values, and uncompromisingly determined to hammer into shape what he loved to characterise as Nepalism, an ideology that could not be mistaken for what obtained in the valley down south.

On 14 March 1955 Mahendra, father of two sons, took an oath to serve Nepal as its King. He was frugal of his time and money, not expansive like his father. He was rather reserved and taciturn of speech. He had a taste for literature, also a good ear for music. He did not have a formal education like his father. But the people of Nepal knew him to be gifted with a strong will, and not a little intelligence and sophistication. His subsequent management of the affairs of his realm amply substantiated this. He had strong likes and dislikes, but he was by nature a forgiving man. He kept his own counsel, and his attitude to India lacked the warmth his father had in abundance.

King Mahendra's first major political move was to convene a conference of the country's various political parties and social organisations, the guiding motivation of which was "to bring my countrymen together around a conference table in an effort to shape the destiny of Nepal." Addressing the conference on 8 May 1955, he said: "Before this conference I would repeat a remark that I have often made . . . Four round years have passed since democracy was brought in . . . During this period the government has been run by several cabinets of ministers from several political parties turn by turn and the number of such ministers are now about 30 . . . When every new cabinet was formed, for the first two of three months of bickerings and in the following two or three months deliberations for the dissolution of the cabinet would go on. . . . Concrete achievements could not ensue from such a state of affairs. Contrarily, people began laughing in their sleeves."

The state of affairs in the kingdom was indeed murky at that time. Organised political life appeared to be disintegrating and the party system stood much discredited. There was no active politician except. B.P. Koirala, who did not seem to hold his reputation cheap. Corruption in political life was not an exception and almost every political party had been smeared by it. It is no figment of imagination that, in the closing days of King Tribhuvan, "corruption and nepotism had acquired a magnitude never known before in the history of Nepal . . . the reputation of no government servant up to the Prime Minister himself was unsullied."

Having pinpointed the affliction that he believed ailed Nepal, the King declared that "under no circumstances whatsoever am I prepared to lose the democratic gains already achieved . . . At the same time I am very eager to unload the burden of administration that has fallen so directly upon my shoulders at a suitable quarter to be found by your unanimous or majority opinion and recommendations. I am emphatic that I am quite unable to be a pensive onlooker of the ruination of the country in the name of democracy." King Mahendra of course did not end his peroration on a negative note. In the given context, he was convinced that a "general election is the crying need of the hour. Without such an election, assessment could not at all be made regarding the magnitude of popularity of any political party. I am much effortful in this regard and have announced that the date for the general election could be fixed in a matter of three months' time.

A careful reading of the King's message would indicate that: he had not, despite his severe indictment of the political parties and their patently dismal performance, closed his mind so far as the parliamentary system of government was concerned; he was determined not to concede the Nepali Congress claim—until a general election bore this out—that it was the largest political party and should therefore be allowed to form a government. Subsequent developments corroborated this. Between his assumption of power and the first general election four years had slipped away, and this was not a very short period. In it the King tried a number of experiments in forming governments apart from the spells of direct Palace rule. But he saw to it that the Nepali Congress was kept out of the corridors of power.

One of the most fateful periods of recent Nepalese history started with a brief spell of the King's personal rule. When he ascended the throne the country did not have a "popular" government, M.P. Koirala having been obliged to relinquish office earlier. Between then and May 1959 Nepal had three nominated governments and two spells of direct rule. King Mahendra's choices as prime minister had a limited brief. For instance it would be preposterous to suggest that Tanka Prasad was nominated to this post because of his intrinsic worth or because of the strength of the party he shepherded. Neither Tanka Prasad nor his Praja Parishad had any better claim to office than any other of the multitude of parties and politicians that crowded Nepal's political mart. What distinguished Tanka Prasad from others however was his pliability. He was ready to plough the sands should the King desire him to do so. Nothing also can explain how his government lasted 18 months, the longest period any government, except the elected B.P. Koirala government, survived between February 1951 and December 1960. That the period of the Tanka Prasad regime was not exactly uneventful is quite another story. Essentially it was that of the King.

King Mahendra seemed to have persuaded himself by now that the Palace constituted the bulwark against all that stood in the path of the country's development in the "great tradition of nation-community, crossing the boundaries of castes, creeds and ethnocentrism." It was imperative in the given context that the Palace should transform itself into an active agent of the country's social, political and economic development. The King exhorted the people "to rise superior to individual or sectional interests and engage ourselves heart and soul in the conquest of hunger and want." And he never tired of using such expressions as "our national destiny," "pride in being a Nepali" and "our national genius."

Nepalese politics took an entirely different turn with the King Mahendra's ascension of the throne. Convinced that "a king . . . can maintain his power if he is astute in internal politics and successful externally," he gave his attention to restructuring the economy, a matter which had received little or no attention in the preceding years. Secondly, King Mahendra had his own plans so far as domestic politics was concerned. They had two aspects: one was to strike a populist stance and open channels of communication with the people. The motivation in this case was a search for allies in his struggle to mould an identifiable Nepalese image out of diverse ethnic groups and cultures. Secondly, his sustained efforts to establish a dialogue with the people, his repeated emphasis on Nepalism, his constant endeavour to be accepted by the people as the symbol of their hopes and aspirations, his unceasing attempts to prevent the political parties from consolidating their position and the refrain on his frequent meet-the-people-tours that his "mission" was to "acquaint myself with the grievances and difficulties confronting my people in the different zones and districts under existing conditions"—all this was of a piece with his strategy of ensuring that the monarchy retained its control of the commanding heights of the Nepalese polity. Thirdly, he initiated a well-planned move to expand the scope and content of the country's hitherto limited contact with the world outside. One of the major considerations which determined his policy, to open as many windows on the world as possible, apparently was to lesson Nepal's dependence on India.

To take the last first. For an understanding of King

Mahendra's approach to international politics it might be helpful to recall once again that, until the advent of Prithvi Narayan, Nepal did not have to bother overmuch about the problem of having formal state-level contacts abroad. The people in the Terai lowlands and in the Kathmandu Valley, the firstnamed particularly, had their social, religious and economic traffic with India. With Prithvi Narayan started Nepal's serious exercise in foreign policy. The basic premise of this was that the country could not afford a foreign policy which ignored the geo-political reality of its location between two giant neighbours, China in the north and India in the south.

There was a deviation from this when the Ranas came to rule the roast. As Major-General Padma Bahadur Khatri. Nepal's Foreign Secretary, put it, "for over a hundred years Nepal's foreign policy was to serve the British interest in the subcontinent." After the exit of the British this "client-state relationship" came to an end and independent India recognised Nepal's sovereignty. At the same time it was given out that India-Nepal ties fell within the purview of what was described as a "special relationship." It was this "special relationship theory," according to Padma Bahadur Khatri, "that created unnecessary bitterness between India and Nepal in the early fifties."

The arrival of King Mahendra on the scene "marks the beginning of a new era in the foreign relations of Nepal," according to Foreign Secretary Khatri. The determinants of the kingdom's foreign policy orientation could easily be identified if it is remembered that "the British were no longer in the subcontinent of India. China in the north was emerging as a power to be reckoned with." King Mahendra did not delay in entering into negotiations for diplomatic ties between China and Nepal, the spadework for which had been started sometime before the death of King Tribhuvan. On 1 August 1955 the two countries agreed on this issue. In September 1956 an agreement on Tibet was formalised ahd Nepal gave up the privileged status it had so long enjoyed in Tibet.

There was nothing very surprising about this. The climate for it had been generated by the post-Bandung spread of amity and fraternity, and the King's shrewd sense of statecraft and predilection for Nepalism. In June 1954, India and China reached an agreement recognising "Tibet as an integral part of China." Less than a year later the Asian-African conference at Bandung produced the Pancha Sheel document, embodying the lofty principles meant to guide relations between nations which participated in the conference. As a result, the attitude of many non-communist Asian governments to China underwent a radical change. It was thus in the fitness of things that Nepal and China should not stay apart diplomatically.

The argument had another side too. Other considerations apart, the King wanted to have as many strings to his diplomatic bow as possible, Nepal's overwhelming dependence on India, both economic and political, the compulsion of referring even inconsequential internal political matters to New Delhi and the evident Indian influence on the life of the country were galling to not a few Nepalese, not excluding King Mahendra. It was not quite comforting to be reminded on and off by Nehru that India was "intensely interested in the stability of Nepal from the point of view of our own security, quite apart from Nepal's," and that "where the question of India's security is concerned, we consider the Himalayan mountains as our border." The Indian Prime Minister apparently could not be faulted for this. After all, Article II of the India-Nepal Treaty of Peace and Friendship of 27 July 1950 provided for India's special relationship" with Nepal. The only way to counteract this was to take full advantage of the country's strategic location, and this is precisely what Kathmandu did when it elected to establish diplomatic ties with Peking.

This was not a peculiar phenomenon. King Mahendra's diplomatic exercise resembled what some of his predecessors had done, especially when they thought that Nepal was getting uncomfortably close to either of its big neighbours. Historical memory dies hard and the King had only to hark back to what had happened in the recent past. It did not take long for him to appreciate the need to correct the imbalance that had crept into the country's foreign policy, albeit without any change in its fundamental direction of nonalignment and friendly relations with all. The King did not have to travel far back in history to recall that before the Ranas took over "whenever relations with the British reached a critical stage, the Nepalis did their utmost to dramatise their relationship with China to the British."

The succession of events seemed to convince the King that he was not following a wrong line of action. In October 1956. Prime Minister Tanka Prasad went to Peking to be rewarded with an aid and assistance agreement. The promised aid amounted to Rs. 60 million, not a small sum considering the disquieting state of the Nepalese economy. As if to counterweigh this Chinese diplomatic thrust, the President of India, Dr. Rajendra Prasad paid a state visit to Nepal in the second half of October. The Indian President emphasised the point that "any threat to the peace and security of Nepal is as much a threat to the peace and security of India. Your friends are our friends and our friends yours." That conceivably was not a very endearing statement to King Mahendra Peking of course did not let things drift. Towards the end of January 1957, Chou En-lai made his way to Kathmandu. The Chinese, Prime Minister reassured the Nepalese that "Nepal and China are blood brothers and nothing can poison this relationship." Not much inside knowledge was called called for to decipher the meaning of this statement.

It would be unwarranted to conclude that India took exception to Nepal's having formal diplomatic ties with China. Or that China was bent upon queering India's pitch in Nepal, at any rate at this point. There is no lack of evidence to support this. Others besides B.P. Koirala might be quoted to bear this out. To the author's query whether New Delhi had reservations regarding Nepal-China diplomatic relations, B.P. Koirala said: "No. I discussed it with Nehru and he said that Nepal could not afford either to antagonise or to remain isolated from any contact with China." As for the Chinese, Koirala said: "I met Chou En-lai . . . when he visited Nepal in

1957. . . . I was with Chou En-lai for three hours and two things he said: first, they were not going to do anything that would harm the interest of India. Second, they did not want to disturb the special relationship that existed between India and Nepal."

The King's concern over the nation's economic life was quite consonant with his total scheme of things. After the revolution national politics had been in a flux, and the impact of this on the economy was all too evident. Pre-occupied with ensuring its mere survival, no government in Kathmandu could get a scheme to reorganise the economy even started. Whether by way of planning or otherwise, no fresh ground had been broken by those who wielded power in the years between 1951 and King Mahendra's accession. In fact, during this period "the economic conditions of the country persisted more or less in the same state of stagnation . . . though the problems of economic planning and development had all along been a popular subject of discussion both within and outside the government."

To get an idea how colossal the problem of economic reconstruction was, it should be recalled that the economy revolved round agriculture, and its system of farming was probably among the world's most inefficient. The *birta* holders owned about two-thirds of all land, reducing the tiller of the soil to the status of a bonded labourer. Organised industry did not exist. The country's total capacity to generate power amounted to about 4250 kilowatts and was restricted to Kathmandu and Biratnagar. It imported practically all its requirements of manufactured consumer goods—from baby food to safety pins—from India. No more than 2 per cent of the population was literate, and there was one doctor for every 170,000 inhabitants.

This state of affairs apparently mocked at the proud King's desire "to make Nepal occupy its rightful place in the comity of nations." Determined to change objective conditions to attain his aims, Mahendra inducted Nepal into the age of planned development. The first five-year plan (1956-61), which had been taking shape for some time, was formally announced. Subarna Shumsher was not being merely polite when he observed, in his capacity as Deputy Premier and Finance Minister, that "with the accession of His Majesty King Mahendra to the throne the period of development was also ushered in." It was indeed a great moment when the King announced that, since he was "eager to see my (8.4 million) people well-housed, well-fed and well-clad, endowed with good education, health and other needed facilities to the maximum extent and within the minimum time limit, a five-year development plan is being formulated . . . it is hoped that the plan will clearly reflect the endeavours being made for the general welfare of the people and the all-round development of the country."

The first plan aimed at an outlay of Rs. 330 million on the part of the government. Of this amount, government was expected to provide Rs. 170 million, while India and the US would provide Rs. 100 million and Rs. 25 miilion respectively as aid. There also was the promise of Rs. 60 million of Chinese aid after the conclusion of the agreement of October 1956. Thus it was expected that nearly 75 per cent of the total plan outlay would be taken care of by foreign aid and assistance.

Aid from abroad has played a not insignificant role in Nepal's economic development. Though its own needs are great, India has all along topped the list of donor countries. Between Nehru's observation on his June 1951 visit to Kathmandu that if Nepal requested "our help in, say, technical or other spheres, we will do our utmost to be useful to you, but we never want to interfere" and the commencement of the uninterrupted flow of Indian aid in 1953 some two years elapsed. The Americans also arrived on the scene quite early and established the US Technical Co-operation Mission in January 1952. After King Mahendra's visit to Moscow in June 1958, the Soviet Union concluded an aid agreement with Nepal, promising thereby some 7.5 million dollars by way of assistance. Some other countries, as well as the United Nations, also extended a helping hand to the kingdom.

The country's crying need was revamping its agrarian system. It was readily acknowledged by the formulators of official economic policy that the "present generation in Nepal, as in many other countries, has inherited an agrarian system which fails in important respects to protect the rights and interests of those who work in land." The hard logic of the Nepalese economy required that land reforms should get priority over everything else. No meaningful reforms in the land system could however be effected without the abolition of the *birta* system. But there was a wide gap between the desires of the planners and reality. The plan did "not envisage any tangible reform proposals" so far as the land system was concerned. It gave scant attention to industrial development, the allocation for this being a meagre 7.8 per cent of the total outlay. Considering the resource constraints on the government, this was probably unavoidable.

Along with his efforts to resuscitate the economy, King Mahendra strove hard to direct the course of the kingdom's politics according to his own plan. Whether on the issue of convening a constituent assembly to frame a constitution or on that of allowing the Nepali Congress to form a government until the promised general election, he held his ground firmly. He held frequent conferences with the political parties, maintaining an almost interminable dialogue with the country's leading politicans, not excluding B.P. Koirala. But he took care not to concede anything that might contradict his scheme of political strategy. He saw to it that the political parties were kept on tenterhooks, and at the same time did not stray too far from the centre of power, the monarchy. In fine, the political parties and their leaders were obliged to depend on his charity.

The Nepali Congress had all along been claiming the right to form a government on the ground that it was the largest political party. But King Mahendra would not agree. Sometime before K.I. Singh was appointed Prime Minister, the King told B.P. Koirala, who in turn told the write, that the Congress would be asked to "form a government . . . I said: 'If you want to include the Nepali Congress, if you want the Nepali Congress to form a government, you should call Subarna Shumsher to do it.' He said that he would like to discuss with me the names of ministers to be included in the cabinet. I told him that it would be better to discuss such matters with Subarna Shumsher because he would be the Prime Minister-designate. He said: 'All right. But I would like to instruct your men not to harm the interest of the monarchy or cause disaffection against it.' Subarna Shumsher was invited for a talk by the King and we were expecting that Subarna Shumsher would be authorised to form a government. Instead he, the King, sent me a personal letter saying: 'My dear B.P., I am sorry to tell you that I have decided to make some other arrangement. Since you said that your party is the largest party. I thought it would be more honourable for you and for me also to call upon your party, after it comes out victorious in the election, to form a government. I hope the decision would not be resented by you or be inconvenient to you.' And immediately K.I. Singh was asked to form a government. All through the three or four days programmes, policies and such things were discussed and came to naught. That is how he functioned. He always kept us at arm's length and at the same time he kept a carrot dangling before us."

When it came to the ticklish issue of framing the kingdom's constitution, King Mahendra won hands down. That was one of his biggest triumphs. Apprehending that a constituent assembly elected on the basis of adult franchise might not frame the type of constitution he would prefer, the King had things so manoeuvred that the political parties, not excluding the Nepali Congress, were obliged to approve his actions. Much to their chagrin, they had to accept the constitution as a gift from the Palace.

The King outwitted everybody, his source of strength being the traditional loyalty of the army, the people's attachment to the monarchy, and the immaturity, expediency and opportunism of the personality-centred political parties. Even the Nepali Congress, despite its hard core of idealism, failed to checkmate his move. He had plenty of friends in the kingdom's political parties, the Nepali Congress not excluded.

On 16 March 1958 King Mahendra appointed a Constitution Drafting Commission enjoining it to prepare a "constitution suitable to the genius of our country." Besides its chairman, Bhagwati Prasad Singh, it consisted of two Nepali Congress leaders, Hora Prasad Joshi and Surya Prasad Upadhyaya, Gurkha Parishad (formerly Gurkha Dal) president Randhir Subba and the Law College principal Ram Raj Pant. The commission also engaged a British constitutional law expert, Sir Ivor Jennings, to advise it. The draft it prepared was approved by the Council of Ministers which the King had appointed on 15 May 1958 and which included a representative each of the Nepali Congress, Gurkha Parishad, Rashtriya Congress and Praja Parishad, and two independents. The Nepali Congress leader Subarna Shumsher was chairman of the Council of Ministers.

While presenting the Constitution to his people, on 12 February 1959, the King emphasised that it was "designed to promote the welfare of this generation and also of those to come and deemed suitable for this ancient land of ours." King Mahendra had every reason to stand foursquare by it, for it was framed along lines he had drawn up and made the monarchy the keystone of the power structure. The 77-article Constitution ensured certain justiciable fundamental rights, a bicameral legislature and an independent judiciary. At the same time it unequivocally guaranteed that "sovereignty continues to reside in the King and not in the people or Parliament."

This evidently was contrary to what King Tribhuvan had promised and what the Nepali Congress had clamoured for all these years. King Tribhuvan had solemnly pledged that the nation would give itself a constitution through its elected representatives. The Nepali Congress had unequivocally declared that it would not rest content with anything short of a constitution framed by a properly elected constituent assembly. Yet when it came to the crunch the Nepali Congress, not to speak of the other political parties and groups, failed to stay the course. The Nepali Congress accepted the Constitution. So did the others. Why the Congress chose not to make a stand against the King was sought to be explained years later by D.K. Sahi, a junior minister in the B.P. Koirala Cabinet, in the columns of *Nepal Today*, a mouthpiece of the emigre Nepali Congress activists. According to Sahi, "there was strong resentment against the Constitution which came as an award from the King. They thought that it would be a derogatory step on the part of the Congress to step down from its original demand of a constituent assembly, but accepted it on the ground that a congenial . . . atmosphere in the long run would definitely promote democracy rather than provoking the King to use his discretionary power for uprooting democracy."

At long last King Mahendra decided that his people should get what they had staged a revolution for and what they had since been asking for. On 18 February 1959 the Nepalese woke up to participate in an event the like of which their history had never before recorded Commanded by their sovereign, the people trooped to the polls to give themselves a parliament of their choice.

Starting on 18 February, the first general election ended on 3 April. Voting was staggered for administrative and other reasons. Ten political parties and groups participated in the election, and of them the Nepali Congress, Gurkha Parishad and the Communist Party were relatively important. A total of 518 candidates contested the election under one party banner or another, while 268 took the field as independents. The table below is self-explanatory.

In its election programme the Nepali Congress emphasised "change in the rural relationship. . . . We said that there should be land redistribution . . . land should belong to the tiller and none should be allowed to own more than 25 bighas (about eight acres) . . . since land was the most important item of national wealth the government should take great interest in its proper utilisation.i' B.P. Koirala said that the party did not have much of an industrial policy. "What we wanted to do was to set up small-scale industries with the help of local capitalists and, wherever necessary, with foreign capital—preferably from

Party	Seats contested	Seats won	Percentage of total votes
Nepali Congress	108	74	38
Gurkha Parishad	86	19	17
United Democratic Party (K.I. Singh group)	86	5	10
Communist Party	47	4	7
Praja Parishad (Tanka Prasad group)	46	2	3
Praja Parishad (Bhadrakali Mishra group)	36	1	3
Independents	268	4	16

Source: Election Commission Reports

India." On inquiry whether the party's programme was socialist, he replied that it was "not, because the conditions in the country were not at all suitable for that. We did not have any economic base for a socialist programme. . . . I should say that what we wanted was that the state should provide direction but must not get directly involved in any execution of economic policy . . . the state should also build up an infrastructure . . . and I wanted the government to impose restrictions on what might be called non-productive production."

By an overwhelming majority, the people of Nepal authorised the Nepali Congress to act on their behalf. The party's past record of struggle and its pledge to carry through a modestly forward-looking programme were convincing enough for the people to give it an unqualified mandate to rule the country for five years. This probably was not very surprising. What was however surprising was the fact that the conservative Gurkha Parishad emerged as the largest oppositon group with 19 seats in Parliament, while the Communist Party got as few as four. Another surprising aspect of the election was the defeat of the leaders of various parties except the Nepali Congress. Of the 36 members of the Upper House of Parliament, 18 were elected and the King nominated the rest. Of the elected members the Nepali Congress got 14, the Gurkha Parishad two and the United Democratic Party and the Communist Party one each.

With the 1959 elections Nepal entered the select fraternity of nations which could claim the privilege of a pluralist polity. The political uncertainties which had engulfed the kingdom seemed to have disappeared and the future looked hopeful. True, there were reasons to believe that King Mahendra did not feel happy about this outcome. The election result had created a situation he had not bargained for. His calculations were that no single party would get an absolute majority, and consequently there would be no scope for a one-party government.

Confronted with this unforeseen development, the King paused to take breath. He neither asked the Nepali Congress to form a government nor indicated the line of action he proposed to follow. Clearly he had never before had to face a situation where he did not have the initiative. As B.P. Koirala put it, King Mahendra "was a man who used to brood over plans, think over and mentally execute a plan before it could be actually put in operation. But he had never been in a situation where all his calculations went wrong. So for three months he sat tight. He did not budge an inch. It was as if there had been no election."

That was not the whole story. In the interval between the announcement of the election results and the formation of the Nepali Congress government B.P. Koirala went to the Palace to tell the King that those who were in the know of things had told him that the King feared him as Prime Minister and that explained why he could not make up his mind. "In order to clear that apprehension." Koirala told the author, "I met him and told him that if he wanted he could make Subarna Shumsher Prime Minister. In the present context, when we are faced with the challenge of modernising our society. . . any difference between the monarch and the Prime Minister. . . would be calamitous for the country. I will certainly support any man that he would want as Prime Minister. . . . Then he said: "Who told you that I am against you? Subarna Shumsher is not very active and energetic. I want an energetic person. I am also young.' He further said. 'Subarna Shumsher is slow; he takes time to decide. The country wants dynamic leadership, so I want you as Prime Minister. And that would also give the lie to the prevalent impression that we had differences between ourselves. I shall be happy if you become Prime Minister."

Disappointment notwithstanding, King Mahendra did not strike a false note. He allowed the political process to run its course. On 27 May he proclaimed: "Whereas, it has been found expedient to found democracy on a more solid basis and to raise the standard of living of the masses and to develop the country within the framework of the laws enacted; I have, therefore, by these presents designated Shri Bishweswar Prasad Koirala as the Prime Minister and with his advice have formed a cabinet under him."

APPENDIX

The first amendment of the constitution, 2019 (1967) has annuled Anchal Panchyat Ain 2019 and all the Anchal Panchayats organised under the same Act. As a result of this change "Anchal Sabha Ain 2024" has been published in Nepal Gazette. This act has made some modifications concerning functions, rights and duties of the Anchal Sabha.

The Anchal Sabha comprises members of all Zilla Panchayats of a zone. It will be an ever rolling autonomus and corporate body. A member of Anchal Sabha will retain his membership so long as he is:

(*a*) a member of the Zilla Panchayat,

(*b*) elected to the post of chairman or vice chairman of the Anchal Sabha, or

(*c*) elected to the National Panchayat (during his tenure) and

(*d*) after his term of office as the chairman or vice chairman of the Anchal Sabha or the Rastriya Panchayat to a period when an election for the vaccant seat does not take place.

But a member of Anchal Sabha can resign by addressing

to the chairman. In such a case the resignation will be effective from that very date. In case of the chairman the resignation must be submitted to the Zonal commissioner and in case of vice chairman to the chairman.

The members of the Anchal Sabha will elect one chairman and one vice chairman out of themselves. But no election will be valid if the chairman or vice chairman fails to score 50 per cent of the valid votes. The tenure of office of the chairman and vice chairman will be four years each.

The following conditions must be full filled in order to be a candidate for the post of Chairman or Vice Chairman:

1. He must not be punished for the crime related to election and not less than one year has elapsed since the imposition of such a punishment,
2. He must be a Nepali citizen.
3. He must not hold portfolios as his Majesty's ministers state ministers, assistant ministers or the members of the National Panchayat
4. the area from which he is going to contest is not administered by another district
5. he has not taken membership of the another Anchal Sabha and
6. he is not declared unfit by any law.

The Achal Adalat (court) has right to determine questions concerning election and its validity.

Works and duties: The Anchal Sabha at the end of every year will submit a detailed report to His Majesty's Government and Anchal Samiti (committee) evaluating various works such as political, social economic and cultural launched within its area. The Anchal Sabha will give its opinion after discussing the report presented by the Anchal Samiti.

The meeting of Anchal Sabha will be held according to the need, and its time and place will be decided by the Chairman. The meeting will be presided over by the Chairman in whose absence the vice chairman and in the absence of the vice chairman by the man selected among the members themselves. If one—third members of the Anchal Sabha ask in writing the chairman has to convene the meeting within 15 days., If the chairman fails to do so the vice chairman has to call the meeting within another 15 days, Even if the vice chairman fails to do it the oldest member of the Sabha can call the meeting within next 15 days. The meeting of the Anchal Sabha will be held only when 51 per cent of the total members do attend in it. Every member of the Anchal Sabha must be notified two days ahead. The decision of the Anchal Sabha must be ratified by two-third majority. The chairman has got only casting vote in case of a tie. The meeting of the Anchal Sabha, in general will be held at the administrative centre of the zone.

The chairman or the vice chairman can be out voted by two-third majority of the members. But in the proposal calling for such a dismissal at least one-third members must sign. But the chairman or the vice chairman has right to defend the allegation either virbally or in writing or in both. The vice-chairman will preside over the meeting when the vote of no—confidence against the chairman will take place and in case of no-confidence against both chairman and vice chairman it will be presided over by a mutually agreed member.

If a suit were to be filed against a person on the decision of Anchal Sabha, according to prevailing rules and regulation of Nepal Chairman Vice-Chairman or the member of Anchal Sabha may present in the court in person, or send his representative or give account in writing. If a Chairman, Vice Chairman or the member is detained on any charge, such information must be sent in writing to the Anchal Samiti through Zonal Commissioner.

His Majesty's Government from time to time can inspect or appoint any body to inspect all moveable and immoveable wealth properties and related papers of the Anchal Sabha and give necessary direction.